Rhinegold Study Guides

A Student's Guide to AS Music

for the **OCR** Specification
2001–2004

by

Paul Terry, Chris Batchelor and David Bowman

Edited by
Lucien Jenkins and Monica Leiher

R·

Rhinegold Publishing Ltd
241 Shaftesbury Avenue
London WC2H 8TF
Telephone: 020 7333 1721
www.rhinegold.co.uk

Rhinegold Study Guides
(series editor: Paul Terry)

A Student's Guide to AS Music for the AQA Specification
A Student's Guide to AS Music for the Edexcel Specification
A Student's Guide to AS Music for the OCR Specification

A Student's Guide to A2 Music for the AQA Specification *
A Student's Guide to A2 Music for the Edexcel Specification *
A Student's Guide to A2 Music for the OCR Specification *

* To be published May 2001

Rhinegold Publishing also publishes Music Teacher, Classical Music, Opera Now, Piano,
Early Music Today, The Singer, British and International Music Yearbook, Music Education Yearbook,
British Performing Arts Yearbook, Rhinegold Dictionary of Music in Sound.

First published 2000 in Great Britain by
Rhinegold Publishing Limited
241 Shaftesbury Avenue
London WC2H 8TF
Tel: 020 7333 1721

© Rhinegold Publishing Limited 2000

All rights reserved. No part of this publication may be reproduced,
stored in a retrieval system, or transmitted in any form or by any means
electronic, mechanical, photocopying, recording or otherwise,
without the prior permission of Rhinegold Publishing Ltd.

Rhinegold Publishing Limited has used its best efforts in preparing this guide.
It does not assume, and hereby disclaims any liability to any party
for loss or damage caused by errors or omissions in the Guide
whether such errors or omissions result
from negligence, accident or other cause.

You should always check the current requirements of the examination, since these may change.
Copies of the OCR Specification may be obtained from Oxford, Cambridge and RSA Examinations at
OCR Publications, PO Box 5050, Annersley, Nottingham NG15 0DL
Telephone 0870 870 6622, Facsimile 0870 870 6621.
See also the OCR website at http://www.ocr.org.uk/

A Student's Guide to AS Music for the OCR Specification (2001–2004)
British Library Cataloguing in Publication Data.
A catalogue record for this book is available from the British Library.

ISBN 0-946890-89-7

Printed in Great Britain by Perfectaprint (UK) Ltd

No composer believes that there are any short cuts to the better appreciation of music. The only thing that one can do for the listener is to point out what actually exists in the music itself and reasonably to explain the wherefore and the why of the matter. The listener must do the rest.

Aaron Copland

Contents

Introduction	*page* 6
Performing	8
Composing	14
Introduction to historical study	21
Western tonal harmony	27
The orchestra 1780–1830	30
Haydn: Symphony 103 (second movement)	32
Mozart: Piano Concerto in A K488 (first movement) . . .	38
Beethoven: Symphony 5 (fourth movement)	44
Rossini: Overture to *The Barber of Seville*	50
Mendelssohn: *A Midsummer Night's Dream* Overture . .	55
Berlioz: *Symphonie fantastique* (fourth movement) . . .	60
Jazz	66
Louis Armstrong: *West End Blues*	72
Duke Ellington: *Rockin' In Rhythm*	79
Duke Ellington: *Ko-ko*	86
Miles Davis: *Move*	93
Miles Davis: *All Blues*	100
Thelonious Monk arr. Gil Evans: *Straight No Chaser* . .	106

The authors

Paul Terry was director of music at the City of London Freemen's School for 15 years and subsequently taught music technology at Kingston Polytechnic (now Kingston University). He currently works as a music editor, engraver and publisher. He has been a music examiner for more than 20 years and has worked as a consultant to various examination boards. Paul has served as a member of the Secondary Examinations Council and its successor the Schools Examinations and Assessment Council. He was chief examiner for the Oxford and Cambridge Schools Examinations Board (now part of OCR) and he was a chief examiner for London Examinations.

Paul Terry's publications include two books on aural for A-level music, written in collaboration with David Bowman (see below). He is also co-author with William Lloyd of *Music in Sequence, a complete guide to MIDI sequencing* (1991), and its companion volumes, *Classics in Sequence* (1992) and *Rock in Sequence* (1996), and also *Rehearse, Direct and Play: A Student's Guide to Group Music-Making* (1993), all published by Musonix/Music Sales.

Chris Batchelor is a freelance trumpet player and composer who was a founder member of the influential 1980s big band Loose Tubes. Since then he has played with Django Bates, David Murray and Hermeto Pascoal among others, and has recently formed the group Big Air with Americans Myra Melford and Jim Black.

He is also a senior lecturer on the BA jazz course at Middlesex University and is working on new jazz syllabus materials for the Associated Board of the Royal Schools of Music. His article 'Jazz Classics', which deals with the first three jazz works in the OCR specification, appeared in the July 2000 issue of *Music Teacher*.

David Bowman was for 20 years director of music at Ampleforth College where he still teaches. He was a chief examiner for the University of London Schools Examination Board (now London Examinations) from 1982 to 1998. He now spends more time with his family, horses and dogs.

David Bowman's publications include the *London Anthology of Music* (University of London Schools Examinations Board, 1986), *Sound Matters* (co-authored with Bruce Cole, Schott, 1989), *Aural Matters* (co-authored with Paul Terry, Schott, 1993), *Aural Matters in practice* (co-authored with Paul Terry, Schott, 1994), *Analysis Matters* (Rhinegold, Volume 1 1997, Volume 2 1998) and numerous analytical articles for *Music Teacher*. He is a contributor to the *Collins Classical Music Encyclopedia* (2000) edited by Stanley Sadie and author of the *Rhinegold Dictionary of Music in Sound*.

The editors

Lucien Jenkins is the editor of *Music Teacher* magazine. He was a contributor to and consultant for the *Collins Classical Music Encyclopedia*, and is the editor of the *Rhinegold Dictionary of Music in Sound*.

Monica Leiher is head of woodwind at Christ's Hospital School in Horsham, West Sussex.

Acknowledgements

The authors would like to thank Veronica Jamset, formerly chief examiner in music to OCR, for her encouragement and advice so freely offered throughout the preparation of this book. Nevertheless if any errors have been made it is only right to state that these are the responsibility of the authors. We would also like to thank Stuart Hall for his expert transcriptions that form the basis of some of the jazz examples in this guide.

Recordings

Details of CD recordings are believed to be correct at the time of publication. However recording companies frequently delete CDs and then re-release the recordings in different compilations with new catalogue numbers and, just occasionally, a reduction in price! In case of difficulty, good local dealers should be able to locate recordings from the information given in the Discography sections.

For each of the prescribed classical works we have mentioned recordings of performances on period instruments as well as those on modern instruments. If possible try to hear both types of performance. It will be very useful to make comparative studies of contrasted recordings, noting in particular how the instrumental timbres and textures differ.

Important note for students

This guide covers all 12 works that are prescribed for study by OCR in the period 2001–2004. In any one year you have only to study **six** works, three orchestral and three jazz. We have indicated clearly throughout the text which works are prescribed for each exam year, and you should be careful to check that you are studying the right pieces. The six prescribed works for each examination year are:

Exam in 2001	Haydn, Beethoven, Rossini
	West End Blues, Ko-ko, All Blues
Exam in 2002	Haydn, Beethoven, Mendelssohn
	West End Blues, Ko-ko, All Blues
Exam in 2003	Mozart, Beethoven, Mendelssohn
	Rockin' In Rhythm, Move, Straight No Chaser
Exam in 2004	Mozart, Mendelssohn, Berlioz
	Rockin' In Rhythm, Move, Straight No Chaser

However we recommend that you try to find time to read through the information on the music that you will not be studying and that you listen to these pieces. All of the orchestral works are closely related in various ways, as are the jazz works. Thus you will gain useful background information and get the opportunity to broaden your knowledge.

In addition, working through the 'aural' questions for any jazz works that you are not studying will give you valuable additional practice in listening to unfamiliar music for Section A (Aural Extracts) of the *Introduction to Historical Studies* paper.

Introduction

This book is intended to assist students preparing to take the OCR examination in AS Music. Like other *Rhinegold Study Guides* it is intended to supplement, but not supplant, the work of teachers.

We have included many suggestions and tips which we hope will help you do well in performing and composing, but the main emphasis is on preparation for the *Introduction to Historical Study* unit. This is because it is our experience that even candidates who are talented performers and imaginative composers can be very unsure of the responses that are required in written work. It is therefore our aim to help you focus on what is important in this part of the exam, and to help you relate your work in listening and understanding to the music that you perform and compose.

In the chapters dealing with the prescribed works we have outlined the essential information for each piece. The questions during the course of these chapters will help you check your understanding of the context, style and technical features of the music – they are not intended to be representative of actual exam questions. If you have difficulty with these, you will generally find the right answers by rereading the preceding pages. The sample questions at the ends of these chapters are more demanding and should be worked under exam conditions. For examples of the questions that are likely to be encountered in the exam, you should be guided by the specimen and (when available) past papers produced by OCR.

We have included explanations of the main technical terms you are likely to encounter in the set works. If you need further help with these, or with other terminology you encounter during the course, we recommend you consult the *Rhinegold Dictionary of Music in Sound* by David Bowman. This comprehensive resource not only gives detailed explanations of a wide range of musical concepts, but it also illustrates them using a large number of specially recorded examples on a set of accompanying compact discs, thus enabling you to hear directly how theoretical concepts are realised in the actual sounds of music.

The *Rhinegold Dictionary of Music in Sound* is published by Rhinegold Publishing Ltd, ISBN: 0-946890-87-0.

Planning is the secret of success especially if, as is common, you are taking AS as a one-year course. Initial ideas for composing are best formulated during the early weeks of the first term, and plans and practice for performing need to get under way as soon as possible. Preparation for the *Introduction to Historical Study* unit needs to be completed in time to allow for revision and the working of mock exams in the weeks before the actual examination.

For success in work at this level, it will help enormously if you can perceive the many varied connections between the music you hear, the music you play and the music you compose. Understanding the context and structure of music will not only enhance your enjoyment when listening, but will also inform your performing and illuminate your composing. Composing, performing, listening and understanding are all related aspects of the study of music, and this integration of activities is fundamental to the course on which you are embarking.

Warning. Photocopying any part of this book without permission is illegal.

AS Music

You will be studying three units: *Performing, Composing* and *Introduction to Historical Study*. Each of these accounts for one-third of the total mark for the AS Music qualification. Two areas of study (*The language of western tonal harmony* and *The expressive use of instrumental techniques*) permeate all three units.

Performing

There are two parts to the Performing unit:

+ you will have to perform a five- to eight-minute solo recital

+ you will have to choose one of the following three options:
  (i) performing on a second instrument
  (ii) performing in a duet or ensemble, or as an accompanist
  (iii) performing your own composition(s).

Your performances, at which you may have an audience present if you wish, will be assessed by a visiting examiner.

Composing

The Composing unit is also in two parts:

+ you will be assessed on a set of not less than six exercises in which you have added a bass part and harmony to melodies that you have been set by your teacher, using the language of western tonal harmony

+ you will have to choose one of the two following options:
  (i) a composition for between four and ten instruments
  (ii) an arrangement of a lead-sheet.

Your music for either of these options must last not more than three minutes and in both cases you are also required to submit a brief commentary on your work.

Your folio of work for both parts of this unit will be assessed by your teacher and then externally moderated by OCR.

Introduction to Historical Study

For the Introduction to Historical Study unit there will be a two-hour exam paper in three sections:

+ Aural Extracts
+ Prescribed Works
+ Contextual Study.

The details of the specification are correct at the time of going to press, but you and your teachers should always check current requirements for the examination with OCR as these may change.

Key Skills

Key Skills are becoming increasingly important for success at work, entry into higher education and for making the most of everyday life. AS Music offers a number of opportunities for you to develop your knowledge and understanding in five of the six Key Skills: Communication, Information Technology, Working with Others, Improving own Learning and Performance, and Problem Solving. You are therefore recommended to discuss with your teachers the ways in which the work you undertake for AS Music might also be used as evidence for your acquisition and development of skills for these Key Skills units at Level 3.

Warning. Photocopying any part of this book without permission is illegal.

Performing

The recital

The solo recital accounts for 60% of the marks for performing. You will need to plan a programme that lasts between five and eight minutes in which you perform at least two pieces. You can have an audience present at the recital if you find this more natural and helpful – it could be just a small group of friends and fellow students – or you can choose to play privately to the visiting examiner, which will probably make the occasion feel more like an exam.

Choice of music Choosing the right music is of paramount importance. The pieces should allow you to show technical and expressive control as a performer as well as an understanding of the music you play. Remember that some types of music, particularly technical studies and some types of pop music, may focus on only a limited range of techniques and not really give you much of a chance to show what you can do as a performer. The pieces should be typical of the solo repertoire of your instrument and they should show the instrument to its best advantage – arrangements of other music may not do this too well and should only be chosen with caution.

It therefore follows that a programme with some variety is likely to serve you best. This could be achieved by a baroque allegro followed by an expressive romantic slow movement and concluded with a short and humorous modern work, or a lively guitar solo followed by a slow blues and concluded with a driving hard rock number. Whatever you choose, aim for contrasts in style and mood, and try to avoid a succession of all too similar slow movements.

The technical difficulty of the music you choose also needs careful consideration. Easy pieces played musically are much more likely to be successful than difficult pieces marred by hesitations and breakdowns. In order to be able to achieve the highest marks the pieces need to be of grade 4–5 standard or higher (if you do not take graded exams your teacher will help explain what this means). However there is no need to struggle to reach this standard (and risk a potential disaster if it proves too difficult) since you will be given credit for what you can do with the music you offer.

Whatever your technical standard it is better to choose music that you can perform with confidence than to attempt a difficult work which stretches your technique to its limit. A work that is too demanding will leave no leeway for the inevitable nervousness that *will* arise under the conditions of a live assessment. The anxiety and tension it generates will be communicated to the listener, and will inevitably impede your musical interpretation.

Choose music that you enjoy playing, but just be a little careful about well-worn 'party pieces' which have proved successful over the years. Most examiners have heard performances of such works trotted out with considerable dexterity but sometimes little thought or feeling or even musicality. A *little* adrenalin arising from a work which is a challenge, but not an insuperable obstacle, usually enhances the work of even the greatest performers.

If the music is intended to have an accompaniment (as will be the case in most music apart from that for piano and other chordal instruments) then it is important that it should be played with accompaniment otherwise it will sound very incomplete. Try to work with an accompanist who can rehearse with you regularly, or at least on several occasions before the recital. Even the most accomplished accompanist will not be able to let you sound your best if the first time you perform together is at the final recital.

You can observe standard performing conventions by omitting repeats or curtailing long sections of accompaniment, but it is not really acceptable to cut passages because they happen to be too difficult or to stop a piece in the middle because it is too long. If such possibilities arise it is better to choose a different work.

Preparations

Having chosen and studied the programme with your teacher, and practised the pieces to a standard that you feel is acceptable, it is essential that you try out the music under performance conditions – not to your instrumental teacher, parents or anyone else who has heard you working on the music week by week, but to someone who is able to hear the performance fresh. This could be a visiting relative, your fellow students, or a different teacher at your school or college. A small slip or two in performance should not concern you greatly, but if you find you are often hesitating in difficult passages or that the piece completely if unexpectedly breaks down then it is a sign that you may have chosen something which is too difficult. This means that you will need to decide if the work is viable or whether it would be better to make a more realistic choice.

In planning this run-up to the recital always allow several more weeks than you think you need. Illness may curtail practice time, other commitments may prevent rehearsals with accompanists or the date for the arrival of the visiting examiner may be much sooner than you anticipated. Worse still, all three problems may occur to conspire against you!

Try to have a run-through of the music in the venue in which you will be performing. If it is a large hall you will probably find that you need to project the sound and exaggerate the contrasts much more than when practising at home. Conversely if you are playing a loud instrument (brass or electric guitar, for example) in a small room to a lone examiner, you will almost certainly need to limit the louder dynamics. Decide where you are going to sit or stand and check that the lighting is adequate but not dazzling. If you have an accompanist make sure that you have good eye contact without having to turn away from your listeners. If the piano is an upright one it may take some experimentation to find the best position.

If the recital is to be given to an audience you should also spend a few minutes practising walking on and off stage, and deciding how you will react to applause. The audience will be disappointed if you shamble on at the start and rush off at the end. Audiences need plenty of time to show their appreciation: a hurried nod in their direction as you exit will appear clumsy, if not downright rude. If there is no printed programme, it makes a friendly start if you announce the pieces you are going to perform – and if you are playing to a lone examiner this will help break the ice.

Warning. Photocopying any part of this book without permission is illegal.

On the day, make sure you leave time for a warm-up and check that you have spare copies of your music for the examiner to use (candidates who play from memory sometimes completely forget to bring any music). Also check that you have to hand any special apparatus you might need (mutes, guitar foot-stools and so on) to avoid having to make a hasty dash off stage in mid-performance. If you need a music stand check that you know how it is adjusted and secured – collapsing music stands are good for comedy acts but they can seriously undermine your nerve in a recital.

Expect to be a little nervous but remember that the more experience you can get of performing to others during the course, the more natural and enjoyable it will become. Blind panic will only normally set in if the chosen music is under-rehearsed or simply too difficult and this, as we have explained, can be avoided by selection of the most suitable music for your needs and a sensible period of careful preparation.

Performing options

For the remaining 40% of the marks available for performing you will need to choose **one** of the three options below. In each case the programme should last between two and four minutes, and in that time you can choose to play either one or two pieces.

Second study You must perform on a different instrument from the one you used in the solo recital (if you are a singer be assured that the voice counts as an instrument for exam purposes). Apart from the smaller scale of the programme, this option is like the main solo recital and similar considerations apply, including the level of difficulty of the music you choose.

Performing compositions For this option you must perform one or two compositions of your own that are written for the instrument (or voice) that you used in the solo recital. They must have accompaniment for **one** other instrument. It is worth noting that the assessment for this option will focus on the accuracy with which you realise the notation of your composition(s), the degree to which they exploit the technical and expressive capabilities of not only your own instrument but also the accompanying instrument, and your aural awareness and understanding in interacting with the accompaniment.

If you choose this option early planning will clearly be of even greater importance, since you will need to take the above points into consideration when creating and refining your compositions. Remember, though, that while most of the rehearsing can only take place once the composing is reasonably complete, it is extremely useful to try out preliminary sketches with the accompanist to test what works in practice and which ideas might be rejected, improved or exploited further.

Performing with others In this option you can choose to play in an ensemble or a duet, or you could opt to perform as an accompanist. Your part must be clearly distinguishable from the others, so playing second violin in an orchestra or singing in a large choral group is not going to be viable. The best choice might well be a small ensemble (two to five people) since it may prove difficult to get larger groups together for rehearsals and the exam.

Warning. Photocopying any part of this book without permission is illegal.

Tips on performing with others

Choosing the right music is of paramount importance if your ensemble is actually to *enjoy* this activity. There should be plenty of choice if you are able to form a standard ensemble, such as a piano trio, brass quartet, jazz combo or rock group, but there are also many pieces available for more unusual groups.

Your teacher will be able to help you find suitable music and will probably have access to the specialist stocks of music available in the local County Music Library. It is also worth spending a little time researching publishers' catalogues, which you can usually view at a local music shop. There are several music retailers who offer a postal service and who can supply extensive lists of ensemble music of many different kinds, including:

Lovely Music, 17 Westgate, Tadcaster LS24 9JB
Telephone 01937 832946; fax 01937 835696
http://www.lovelymusic.co.uk

June Emerson Wind Music, Windmill Farm, Ampleforth,
York, YO6 4HF. Telephone 01439 788324; fax 01439 788715
http://ourworld.compuserve.com/homepages/JuneEmerson/

Chamberlain Music (choral music specialists), Weyhill, Haslemere,
Surrey GU27 1HN. Telephone 01428 658806; fax 01428 658807
http://www.chamberlainmusic.co.uk

Try to find music that is designed for the instruments you have available. Be aware that some easy arrangements, especially those designed to suit any of a range of different instruments, may have inner and lower parts that will be very dull for your players. They are unlikely to generate enthusiasm in rehearsal, or to give much opportunity for the display of real ensemble skills.

Spending a little time on preparation will make rehearsals much more productive and enjoyable for all the participants. Check that you have parts for each player – spare copies are a useful precaution, since you can almost guarantee that someone will lose or forget their music just before a rehearsal. Make sure that all the parts have bar numbers or rehearsal letters, so you can easily restart a piece in the middle rather than always having to go back to the start. It is also useful to have a supply of pencils (the other members of the ensemble will almost certainly not remember to bring their own) so that decisions made at rehearsals can be marked into the parts.

Performing with others means understanding the important difference between practising and rehearsing:

- **practising** is done by each member of the group, before the ensemble meets for the first time
- **rehearsing** is done by the ensemble, after all of its members have learnt at least the basics of their own individual parts.

Rehearsals should not be a time when individual players practise their parts. If that happens the rest of the group will quickly become bored. Be sure to distribute the music well in advance so that it can be practised before the ensemble meets for the first time, and be very clear about the date, time and venue of the rehearsals.

Warning. Photocopying any part of this book without permission is illegal.

An ensemble that has rehearsed efficiently will also tend to perform with greater confidence. It is best to rehearse in the place where the performance will take place. If that is not possible, at least try to plan how you will sit for the performance and keep to those positions in rehearsal. It is essential that everyone has direct eye contact with everyone else. Sitting or standing in a semicircle often works well, with any large instruments placed further back. If the performance includes a piano, and only an upright instrument is available, it will be important to spend some time experimenting to find a position in which the pianist has a reasonably uninterrupted view of the other performers.

Accurate tuning is vital and it is essential that you get into a routine of taking time to do this thoroughly. Wind players must warm up before tuning, but once this is done it is essential that the rest of the group stays silent while each player tunes. Less experienced players will need to remember that they must adopt a good playing posture and then sound a long note at a moderately loud volume in order to check pitch – a quick toot will not be enough. Wind players should ensure that they sound the note with proper breath support. Tuning should not be hurried, although the process should become slicker by the time of the actual performance.

Finally, before starting to rehearse the music itself, try a few very slow scales in unison, listening carefully to each other's intonation – this exercise will also help give any singers a chance to warm up before they start.

Once the preliminaries are over, it is best to run through as much of the music as possible. Try to get to the end, even if some parts are a bit sketchy, to allow everyone to get some idea of how the piece fits together. After this, the serious work of rehearsal can begin.

Although you will undoubtedly want to concentrate on your own part, remember that the assessment is of your skill in ensemble performance, and that includes the extent to which you are aware of, and respond to, the rest of the group – or to the soloist if you have chosen the accompanying option. Find the focus of the music by discussing its mood and purpose with the other performers, and check that you are all in agreement with the way in which you wish to communicate the music to your audience. This is not just a matter of finding the right tempo. Try to decide the key elements you wish to communicate: rhythmic drive, a dreamy atmosphere, elegant phrasing, dramatic contrasts or subtle blends. Then focus in on the detail of what this means. Rather than agreeing that a passage should sound 'happy' try to decide if you mean boisterous, contented, frivolous, celebratory, cheeky or merely cheerful. If it is 'sad', try to focus on whether this means tragic, doom-laden, nostalgic, angry or solemn. The group is more likely to respond quickly and positively to the right adjective, or the right image, than to a long list of technical instructions that are quickly forgotten.

Ensuring that the parts are together and accurate is only the start of the rehearsal process. Even at an early stage you are likely to need to work on improving contrasts – making *staccato* notes razor sharp and totally unanimous, *pianissimo* passages almost inaudible and *forte* climaxes rich and vibrant.

As rehearsals progress, you will need to work increasingly on the interpretation of the music. The details will depend on the music you have chosen, but you are likely to need to concentrate on:

+ **Good balance**. Performers need to know when their part is at the forefront of the ensemble and when they need to hold back in order to let others shine. Be careful that instruments such as the piano or saxophone don't overwhelm quieter instruments.

+ **Rhythmic vitality**. A performance that is sluggish and lacking a feeling of pulse will be dull. Be specially careful that everyone can feel a unanimous pulse in any slow sections – try a quaver (or even semiquaver) pulse if crotchets don't feel right – and check that dotted and tied notes are really precise.

+ **Expressive phrasing**. Every phrase needs shape and focus. Those with accompanying parts need to listen (without playing) to the main melodic line and then shape their own phrasing to match. Vocal groups should mark breathing points into their music to help ensure unanimity of phrasing. Words must always be clear, but try to avoid intrusive consonants that break the phrasing.

+ **Atmosphere and commitment**. All players should try to share a clear image of the mood they are trying to convey, be it the glittering ballroom of a minuet, the moonlit night of a nocturne or the smokey languor of a blues club.

As you work in increasing detail, remember to pencil into the music all the important points you cover to avoid having to go over the same matters time and again at every rehearsal.

When it comes to the performance the points we made about solo recitals apply equally to ensemble playing. Make sure you have a warm-up before you start. Take care that seating and music stands are in the right position, that lighting is good but not dazzling and, if you are to play to an audience, that you rehearse walking on and off stage and acknowledging audience applause. When you go on remember that tuning should be efficient but not hurried. And once again, if there is no printed programme, it makes a friendly start if, *after* tuning, one of the group announces the ensemble and the piece(s) it is going to play.

Additional reading

Rehearse, Direct and Play by William Lloyd and Paul Terry. *Musonix Publishing*, 1993. ISBN: 0-9517214-3-7.
Available from *Music Sales Ltd.* (Order No. MX 30053, £4.95)

Music Sales Ltd, Newmarket Road, Bury St. Edmunds, Suffolk IP33 3YB.
Telephone: 01284 702600;
fax: 01284 768301
http://www.musicroom.com/

This useful handbook (from which some of the information in this chapter is used, by kind permission of Musonix Publishing) is a student's guide to group music-making of all kinds.

Warning. Photocopying any part of this book without permission is illegal.

Composing takes time and most people find that initial ideas have to be worked over a number of times before a satisfactory shape starts to emerge. Considerable rewriting – perhaps even starting again – should be expected as ideas are tried out with your chosen instrumentalists. It is therefore advisable to start your compositions as early in the course as possible, so that you have time both to reject the ideas that don't work and to refine the ideas that do.

Notation

Your score and parts must be clear and unambiguous, and include all of the details necessary for performance. A well-chosen title can help to make your intentions clear. If you use transposing instruments it is permissible to write them at concert pitch in the score (but the parts will need proper transposition if performers are to make sense of them). However you must use the normal conventions for octave displacment (e.g. piccolo and descant recorder are written an octave lower than they sound, while double bass, guitar and bass guitar are written an octave higher than they sound).

Features such as computer-typeset title pages, colourful artwork and elaborate bindings will gain you no extra marks. Aim for a clear, simple layout with numbered pages clipped together in the right order. Bar numbers, either at the start of each system or every ten bars, are a helpful addition. Remember that the layout of the parts may be dictated by the position of page turns, which should be in places where the performer concerned has a rest of adequate length – and don't forget that players of large instruments such as the double bass will need plenty of time for a page turn.

In the score, staves should be labelled with an instrument name at the start of every system, although abbreviations can be used for this after the start of the piece. When writing more than one system on a page it will help the layout if you leave a blank stave or two between systems. You can use conventional repeat signs in the score to avoid copying out identical sections of music but the score must be complete. Work that consists of melodic sketches and chord symbols, with instructions on how they might be interpreted is not acceptable at this level of music studies.

Computer-generated scores

Computer-generated notation is allowed and can produce very neat results, but there can be many pitfalls, especially if you generate a score from sequencing software. Sequencers are designed to record note lengths very precisely, just as they are played. If those note lengths are then displayed as a musical score, the result can become a performer's nightmare, with a simple crotchet perhaps appearing as triple-dotted quaver followed by a hemi-demi-semi-quaver rest or as a long succession of very short notes tied together. It is not that the software is wrong, but that it is attempting to display note lengths in far too much detail for a performer easily to interpret. Most sequencer software has facilities, such as score quantization, to help achieve more acceptable results, but you will still need to check the output carefully for eccentric note lengths, and unnecessary rests and ties.

Software usually handles pitch better than rhythm, but again you must be on your guard for incorrect accidentals (e.g. A♯ in F major, when the note should be a B♭). Check carefully for anachronisms such as printing low clarinet notes in the bass clef. Excessive leger

> **Warning.** Photocopying any part of this book without permission is illegal.

lines should be avoided, either by using a different clef if appropriate, or by using an 8va sign. In particular, be sure to check that the software is correctly handling parts for instruments whose music should be written an octave higher than it sounds.

Remember that you will probably need to edit in the phrasing and articulation that you require, and to make sure that the staves are labelled with the instruments you intend, and not just track numbers. Most software should be able to produce correct stem directions and accurate beaming (grouping of notes), but again you should check that you have the right settings for the music concerned.

You will also need to know how your software handles repeats. It may well print the music out again in full, when what is really required is a repeat sign or a *da capo* direction, perhaps with first- and second-time bars in order to differentiate different endings.

Most of these problems can be overcome by careful study of the software manual, but remember that it is most unlikely that you will be able merely to press the 'Print' button in order to achieve an acceptably accurate score. If you are lucky enough to have access to high-quality software optimised for music notation the task will be somewhat easier, but will still need very careful checking. OCR makes it clear that, if you use computer-generated notation, you will still be responsible for the accuracy and completeness of the scores you submit. In some cases you may find it quicker, and perhaps more satisfying, to use traditional pen and ink.

Computers can make the task of producing parts from the score very much quicker, but remember that your performers will need page turns in suitable places and players of transposing instruments will require the part to be in the correct key. Also, try to use a decent quality of paper for printing the parts since flimsy computer print-out paper will never stay upright on a music stand.

Checklist

Use the following check list to ensure that you haven't missed any essential points in your score and parts.

- Have you given the work a meaningful title?
- Is there an initial tempo marking?
- Have you remembered the time signature?
- Are all the staves labelled with the relevant instrument?
- Do all the staves have the correct key signature?
- Have all dynamics, articulation and other essential performing directions been included?
- Are all the notes for each instrument playable?
- Are phrase marks and slurs clear? They should always begin and end on specific notes – not on bar lines or between notes.
- Does every bar have the correct number of beats? Checking is tedious but essential if you are to avoid this common fault.
- Have you numbered the bars for easy reference?
- Are there any blank bars? If a part is not playing it should either be omitted from the system or be given whole-bar rests, since blank bars can be ambiguous.
- Have you included a key for any parts, such as drum kit, that use non-standard notation?
- Are all the pages numbered and in their correct order?

Warning. Photocopying any part of this book without permission is illegal.

Finally, remember that you need to include instrumental parts with the score, a recording and a commentary. The last of these can be brief. It is not necessary to explain how you sat down at the piano and discovered the dominant 7th. You need to list the precise passages in the music you have studied (scores, recordings or both) that have influenced your choices of instrumentation. Sometimes it may be a technique from one of the prescribed works or your other listening that you liked and adopted in your own work, but in other cases it may be a more general idea, such as a texture or an atmosphere, in which case you can briefly explain how you developed and expanded it for your own purposes.

Arranging a lead-sheet

If you choose this option you will be expected to develop the single melody line and chord symbols of a lead-sheet into a full arrangement lasting not more than three minutes. Some of the more common formats and structures are discussed later in this book in the chapters on the prescribed works. These pieces can form excellent models for this type of arranging and we have discussed some ideas to help you in those chapters.

In your arrangement you will need to cycle through the head (the melody and chords) several times, probably adding additional material in the form of an intro, coda and linking sections. When using a repeated chord pattern it is important not only to use variation but to use it in an architectural fashion so that the music has shape. The prescribed works will point to some of the ways in which this can be done. You will see that it can often be advantageous to embellish the basic chords with additional notes and sometimes to substitute a chord with something related but slightly different in order to provide variety. You are free to use the given material in any key you wish, and to modify the rhythm and introduce modulation if it strengthens your arrangement.

There is no requirement that your arrangement should be a jazz arrangement – it could be in a variety of pop, blues or dance styles. However study of the prescribed jazz works will point you towards a number of ideas that will work well in any style. For instance you will see that exact repeats of the main melody are rare. It is much more common to vary the repeats or perhaps use just a single motif from the melody and develop it in different ways over the common chord pattern. In almost every case you should notice how such variations arise from, and exploit, the characteristics of the solo instrument(s) concerned. If you yourself are to do this effectively it will need a keen awareness of instrumental techniques as well as time to work with the performers concerned in order to develop your arrangement in the most effective way.

You must create a variety of appropriate bass and rhythm parts from the given material as well as an effective overall structure. If the arrangement is going to make the impact you hope for it must include reasonable variety of texture and you should also consider how additional detail might enhance the final product – carefully notated backing parts that support but don't mask the solo lines, countermelodies and written-out solos. Once again, the prescribed jazz works should provide you with plenty of ideas.

A complete and accurate full score is required for this option (although not a set of parts), so read the earlier advice on notation and make use of the checklist on page 17.

You will need to provide a recording of your arrangement (which may be in reduced or synthesized form if the full resources for your intended instrumentation are not available) and also a commentary. The latter can be brief but it needs to explain how the music you have listened to has influenced your ideas. Try to relate precise passages in the music you have heard to techniques you have adopted and explain how you have modified and reinterpreted these ideas in your own arrangement.

Achieving a good mark

Concentrating on the following three aspects of composing should help you achieve a good mark.

Development of ideas

Many of us stumble across occasional great musical ideas when doodling at the keyboard or singing to ourselves in an idle moment. The difficulty is always what to do next, after that initial bar or that opening phrase. Many promising openings are spoilt by excessive repetition in the bars that follow, leading to too little variety and no sense of alternating areas of tension and rest. Conversely, and perhaps even more commonly, are openings that are followed by too much diversity – so many new ideas in rapid succession that the piece fails to hang together.

The best way out of this dilemma is to study what happens in the music that you know. Start from the pieces you play and the music you listen to, both from the prescribed works and the music you enjoy in your leisure time. Note the techniques used by composers to represent their material in different contexts. Instead of introducing new ideas, take time to explore your opening idea in more depth. Break it up into smaller motifs and try to give these a life of their own before introducing new material. Above all, aim for a balance of unity and diversity in your work.

Control of texture

Most composition examiners would agree that this is the area in which candidates have the most difficulty, and yet varied textures are vital to most types of music. If you assign your melody line to one instrument throughout and condemn the other parts to dull accompanying lines, you risk the wrath of most of your players, the boredom of your audiences and a low mark in your exam.

Try to distribute thematic material among *all* the resources at your disposal, remembering that each instrument in your ensemble can use different parts of its range. Use contrasted dynamics and articulation to help achieve variety. Try to break longer melodies into short motifs that dart from one instrument to another. Accompanying parts will be far more interesting if lugubrious semibreves are replaced with some rhythmic movement or interesting figuration. The use of a countermelody or other simple contrapuntal device can transform an ordinary piece into a work of real interest. Pay particular attention to phrase endings. If phrases often end on a long note try to add some decoration or a link motif in another part to propel the music forwards, or see if the end of the phrase can be overlapped with the start of the next.

> Warning. Photocopying any part of this book without permission is illegal.

Points of tension and relaxation are vital in most music, and such moments need careful planning throughout the piece, especially if you are using a repetitive structure such as may occur in a lead-sheet arrangement. Changes in texture play a vital role in defining points of climax, where a thickening of chords, increase of harmonic pace, rise of melody to a high note, addition of extra parts and increase in rhythmic activity can combine to maximise the impact you intend.

Above all, remember that **rests** are the key to achieving good variety of texture. They are essential if wind players are not to expire before the final cadence, but they are also essential to give relief to the ear. Assign solos to different parts of your texture and don't feel obliged to occupy all the instruments in every bar. Experiment with different combinations, such as a melody in the bass or inner part, and remember that occasional moments of totally unaccompanied melody can be ravishingly beautiful.

Refinement of ideas

You would be talented indeed simply to compose a piece of music and not then need to refine and polish it. At the very least you are likely to have to make adjustments as a result of trialling the work in performance. In addition to matters such as unplayable passages or miscalculated balance, you should be prepared to use a critical ear to identify the passages where the music seems to lose its impetus or direction. Perhaps a long note at a cadence needs to be sparked into life by adding an embellishment in another part, or perhaps a tendency for the piece to sound too sectionalised needs to be corrected by overlapping phrases or adjusting the lengths of sub-phrases.

Gnawing away at the details in order to refine the work is a normal and expected part of the compositional process, but there will also be a time when you should let go. Music is not a science, and you will reach a stage at which further change is likely to be counter-productive and could result in inconsistencies of style that detract from your original conception of the piece.

How much should I write?

The Composer's Handbook by Bruce Cole. *Schott and Co Ltd*, 1996. ISBN: 0-946535-80-9. This is full of ideas and techniques for composing in a wide range of styles, and it covers basic starting-points as well as more extended and advanced work.

Orchestral Technique by Gordon Jacob. *Oxford University Press*, 1931, 3rd edition 1981. ISBN: 0-19-318204-1. An excellent short introduction that is mainly concerned with orchestration but which also contains much useful information on using and combining standard orchestral instruments.

Rock, Jazz and Pop Arranging by Daryl Runswick. *Faber and Faber*, 1992. ISBN: 0-571-51108-2. This useful handbook offers many hints and tips as well as some specific guidance on lead-sheet arrangements.

Most compositions tend to find their own natural length and you will of course be constrained by the three-minute time limit. However a few bars of *adagio* in an unvarying C major that attempts to fill the page by dint of excessive repetition is unlikely to meet many of the criteria for a successful mark.

Composing involves a certain amount of risk, and your efforts are more likely to be successful if you attempt a piece that displays a real sense of character and ambition. For a high mark you need strong, inventive and confidently-shaped materials, a clear sense of structure, and good use of contrast and continuity.

Finally, remember that while a neat and unambiguous score is important, it is not the object of the exercise. There is no need to try to impress by filling it full of Italian directions (English is perfectly acceptable) or by peppering it with a random selection of dynamics and performance directions that have no relation to the musical content. Keep it clear – keep it simple. Some books that you may find useful for reference are listed *left*.

Introduction to historical study

This unit focuses on both areas of study (*The language of western tonal harmony* and *The expressive use of instrumental techniques*) and it thus links with your work in composing. The unit encompasses aural and the study of six prescribed works: three orchestral scores from the late 18th and early 19th centuries, and three 20th-century jazz recordings. There is a single two-hour exam paper in three parts:

1. **Aural Extracts**

You will be given a tape recording and skeleton scores of two musical extracts, and you will be required to answer a series of questions on one of them. These may include:

- writing down parts of the melody or bass that you hear
- identifying chords (triads, inversions and 7ths)
- recognising melodic dissonances
- recognising phrasing
- identifying keys and closely-related modulations
- spotting devices such as dominant pedals and sequences
- recognising techniques of melodic variation, playing techniques and instrumentation.

One of the extracts will be a variation movement from the period 1700–1830 and the other a piece of instrumental jazz or popular music from the 20th century. You will be able to choose which of these two you wish to work on. You may play the tape as many times as you wish, but OCR advises that you spend not more than 40 minutes on this section, which carries 35% of the total marks available for this unit.

2. **Prescribed Works**

There are two questions, both of which must be answered. For the first question you will be given a printed extract (but no recording) taken from one of the three orchestral works you have studied. The questions on this passage will centre on the conventions of notating orchestral music and the expressive effects of the instrumentation in the passage. You will also be asked to identify the location of the extract within the movement from which it is taken and to show an understanding of the main features of the form of the movement. The questions require mainly brief answers and this section of the paper carries 25% of the total marks available for this unit.

In the second question you will be given a recorded extract (but no printed notation) taken from one of the three jazz works you have studied. The questions on this passage will centre on the instrumental and performing techniques, instrumentation and arranging techniques, expressive effects and the approaches to improvising in the passage concerned. You may be asked to compare specific passages and place the extract in the context of the whole piece from which it is taken. Again, the questions require brief answers and this section of the paper carries 15% of the total marks available for this unit.

3. Contextual Study

In the final part of the paper there will be five questions, all centred on the prescribed works. These may require you to discuss the historical background and context of the music or to write about the development and use of relevant instruments and instrumental textures in the pieces. You may be required to discuss arranging, performing and improvising techniques used in the works and perhaps to make comparisons between various aspects of the pieces you have studied.

You will have to answer **one** of these five questions. It will require a longer answer than the earlier questions although not a full-length essay – approximately a single page should prove sufficient to express your ideas. Your answer should be in continuous prose and you should note that the quality of your written communication will be assessed in this part of the paper, although the examiners will of course be primarily interested in how thoroughly you answer the question. This final section accounts for the remaining 25% of the total marks available for this unit.

Most of the rest of this guide is devoted to a detailed survey of each of the prescribed works. We have included all 12 works set over the next few years, but remember that in any one year you study only six (three orchestral scores and three jazz recordings) so check the exam dates at the head of each chapter carefully – but also try to read through the other chapters since they will help your understanding of context and development.

Each chapter starts with information about the work's context and a brief overview of its form. This is followed by a detailed listening guide which focuses on instrumentation and instrumental techniques. There are a number of questions designed to help you check your understanding of the topic as well as suggestions for further reading and a selected discography for each work. We have also included some ideas for group work and composing, and at the end of each chapter you will find sample questions to give you some exam practice, particularly in your final weeks of revision.

In the chapters on the jazz works we have also included some short 'aural practice' questions to help you focus your listening and develop some of the skills needed for the 'aural extracts' in the first part of the exam paper. However you will need more practice than we have space to provide in a guide of this length. The following two books give detailed help in developing aural skills, including dictation tests and the recognition of compositional features in musical extracts. Both come with specially produced CDs, and the first includes selected material from the jazz and pop repertoire. Although not all of their contents are applicable to the current OCR specification, you should find within their pages much to help your development of aural perception when listening to music.

Aural Matters by David Bowman and Paul Terry. *Schott and Co Ltd*, 1993. ISBN: 0-946535-22-1.

Aural Matters in Practice by David Bowman and Paul Terry. *Schott and Co Ltd*, 1994. ISBN: 0-946535-23-X.

Why write about music?

This is a very pertinent question for anyone taking an advanced course in music. After all, it is obvious that the prime purpose of music is to be *heard* rather than written about. Or is it? In purely physical sense we do of course *hear* music, but is that all? We hear traffic noise, but we usually try not to *listen* to it. With music, on the other hand, we tend to *listen* because it engages our attention. Sometimes we listen to music simply to let pleasurable sound wash over us, but at other times listening seems to reveal patterns and ideas, or to suggest and enhance moods or emotions. These are matters that can often appear difficult or complex to write about, not least because music seems to express such feelings so much more directly than the written word.

One of the joys of music is that it can be simultaneously understood at many different levels. You really don't need to know anything at all about Beethoven's third symphony to be stirred by the heroic ideas that emanate from the music when you hear it. But this leaves us with nagging questions as to *how* it does this and *why* listeners to the symphony respond to it in remarkably similar ways. Why does Beethoven's seventh symphony *not* sound heroic, but instead makes us want to get up and dance? Why does one top-ten hit sound corny while another makes us want to play it time and again? Why does one piece of music that we are learning to play fully engage our interest while another bores us stiff? By studying the music in depth we can begin to answer such questions and to find out how the music actually works.

Studying the context in which music was written can help us to see why certain combinations of instruments were used at certain times, why various technical devices were used by some composers but not by others, and how the demands of different consumers of music – be they aristocratic patrons, government-funded arts councils or even the record-buying, concert-going public – resulted in music adopting the forms and genres it has during different periods of history.

As we explore below the surface of worthwhile music of any kind, more and more detail starts to emerge, detail that we may have scarcely heard in the past, but that now we listen for. New interconnections emerge each time we listen, new detail that previously escaped our attention is now revealed to have significance to the whole. And thus it is that we begin to understand how and why one work of art can be universally recognised as a masterpiece, while another may do no more than fleetingly engage our attention.

Once our own listening experience is enhanced in this way, we can see how studying music can illuminate performing. It can help us bring to the attention of our audiences the overall architecture of the music, as well as the myriad of fine detail and the web of interconnections we have discovered, thus enhancing their own listening experience. Understanding music in detail can equally inform our work as composers, helping us to explore subtle ways of structuring our music and suggesting ways in which additional layers of detail can reveal themselves to the listener at each new hearing.

Studying music

From the very start of your course you need to be clear that the focus of your studies must always be the music itself. It cannot be too strongly emphasised that your work should be based on the *sound* of the music. Why does Mozart sound different from Duke Ellington? What do the players do to make it sound different?

Some students seem to go to unnecessary lengths to avoid tackling the music head on. They learn long lists of dates, or the number of symphonies Haydn wrote, or quotations of what other people say about the music. Background information *directly related to the piece concerned* can be important in understanding the context of the music – why it was written in the way it was – but make sure that your main focus of attention remains on the music itself: the broad outlines of its form and use of musical language, and the detailed study of its expressive use of instrumentation.

Examiners will be looking for well-focused responses that answer the precise questions posed and, in the last part of the paper, that are supported by specific references to the music itself. This cannot be done by trying to memorise 'prepared answers' that you hope might somehow fit the question, like an embarrassed politician in a television interview. Nor can it be done by responding in vague generalities about what a splendid and moving piece you think you have studied.

So the key to success in this unit is to get to know the music very thoroughly, and to understand why, when and how it was written. Before starting to study each work play it often enough to begin forming an internalised image of its sound, just as you can probably already imagine the sound of pieces you have learnt to play or sing. Try to broaden your knowledge of musical repertoire by listening to and studying other music related to the prescribed works.

Terminology In your studies you are likely to encounter various musical terms that are new to you. These will make much more sense if you ensure that, whenever appropriate, you understand the *sound* to which they refer – don't just rely on dictionary definitions, but relate the term or concept to your own composing and playing.

Try to be sure that you really have correctly understood terms that you might have been using for some years. Examiners often come across references such as 'the theme of bar 1 is imitated in bar 96', where a candidate meant that it was repeated, or 'Haydn sequenced the first theme', when they meant that he used a sequence, not an 18th-century sequencer. If in doubt about the correct technical term, try to explain what you mean in plain but precise English.

Note taking Get into the habit of keeping clear, well-ordered notes. They will be much more useful than just rereading old essays when it comes to revision. Be selective and highlight anything that seems important. Leave plenty of space, so you can make additions later. Making pencil notes in the score is also very useful, providing your teacher agrees to this.

Your main sources of information will be recordings, scores, guides such as this and reference books, but remember that your best source of information is your teacher. Don't just sit back and take reams of notes, but try to develop a questioning approach. Ask for clarification of anything and everything you don't understand. Your teacher won't mind – in fact, he or she will be delighted if you show an interest in the work and in improving your own performance.

In the final part of the paper you will need to write a more extended answer than is required by the earlier questions. It is important to develop a clear style and to make sure that you:

+ understand the question you have chosen
+ give a relevant and logical answer to it
+ provide evidence for your statements.

Understanding the thrust of the question is essential. A common fault is the answer that quotes the question and then immediately goes off at a tangent in order to provide a 'prepared answer' – one that was really destined for some quite different question. Even if you offer a lot of accurate information, failing to answer the specific question will inevitably lose many marks.

Avoid digression. You do not need to write an essay; you do need to be concise. There is no need for opening paragraphs to set the scene, or to describe the composer's life or other works. Dive straight in and tackle the subject head on, with one short paragraph on each of your main points. If you find your answer starting something like this, you have almost certainly got off on entirely the wrong foot:

> Haydn was born in 1732. He was a classical composer who wrote at least 104 symphonies and many sonatas. He was born in Austria and his father was a farmer and a wheelwright. He had a musical brother and they were both choristers at the cathedral in Vienna, where Haydn was said to have had a very good voice.

It should be obvious that this tells us nothing about the *sound* of Haydn's music. For a good mark you should be able to highlight matters of significance, and to use your knowledge to interpret and explain bare factual detail. Try to avoid personal opinions of a general nature, such as stating how much you like the piece. If you do feel it appropriate to include a personal reaction, make sure that it is backed up by evidence from the music, e.g. 'the start of the development sounds doom-laden *because* …'.

It is usually best to avoid long sentences because they can easily become so convoluted that the point gets lost. Organise your material into a logical order and avoid adding extra points as asterisked footnotes or additions in the margin.

Citing evidence for your arguments will give authority to your answer and your main source of such evidence will usually be the music itself. Try to refer directly to something in the music to illustrate each of your main points. For example, instead of merely writing …

> Mozart often uses thin textures.

illustrate your point with an example …

> Mozart's preference for thin textures can be heard in the very first entry of the piano, which uses just a two-part texture.

Contextual study

Symphony No 103 (second movement) Haydn

Prescribed for examination in 2001 and 2002

During his long and successful career Franz Joseph Haydn (1732–1809) saw the orchestra develop from a modest group of strings, oboes and horns to the large double-wind orchestra described on page 30. Over the same period the symphony was transformed from a lightweight three-movement entertainment to a substantial and complex work of four carefully balanced movements, becoming the principal type of music played by these newly enlarged orchestras.

Haydn was a key figure in these developments. For much of his life he was director of music to the Hungarian Prince Esterházy at a magnificent palace 50 kilometers south-west of Vienna. Here he had every facility to perfect his craft. He said to his friend and biographer, Georg Griesinger,

> I could experiment, observe what created an impression and what weakened it, thus improving, adding, cutting away, and running risks. I was cut off from the world … and so I had to become original.

Haydn may have felt remote at the palace on the Austro-Hungarian border, but his reputation in the rest of Europe was growing through publications in Vienna, London and Paris. When Prince Nikolaus Esterházy died in 1790, a violinist and concert promotor named Peter Salomon immediately engaged Haydn to come to London and to compose six new symphonies for the extended visit. These were an instant success and Haydn was engaged to write six more (Nos 99–104) for a further visit in 1794–5. These 12 works, known as the 'London' symphonies, are the pinnacle of Haydn's achievement as 'father of the symphony'. Each builds simple, accessible musical ideas into strong symphonic structures, full of wit, that explore the sonorities of the large and accomplished orchestras available to Haydn in the concert rooms of London.

The 'Drumroll' Symphony

Haydn's Symphony No 103, nicknamed the *Drumroll* because the first movement begins with a roll on a kettledrum, was given its first performance in the concert hall of the King's Theatre, London on 2 March 1795. The orchestra, jointly directed by Haydn at the piano and Salomon as leading violinist, was very large for the time, with 40 strings and 20 wind players. The latter figure suggests that the eight woodwind parts must have been doubled, at least in *tutti* passages in which the whole orchestra was playing.

Haydn uses a full woodwind section in the rest of the symphony but the clarinets do not play in the third movement.

Form

The symphony consists of four movements, of which the second is a set of variations on two alternating themes, a form often called a **double theme and variations**. The other movements are in the key of E♭ major, but the slow movement provides an area of contrast within the symphony by being centred in the relative minor key of C minor, with substantial sections in C major.

This interplay between minor and major versions of the same key is established by the two themes, the first in C minor (bars 0–26) and the second in the parallel tonic key of C major (bars 26–50). Each of the two variations similarly consists of a minor section followed by a major section. It is easy to tell the two themes apart,

Theme	C minor	Bars 0–26
	C major	26–50
Variation 1	C minor	50–84
	C major	84–108
Variation 2	C minor	108–134
	C major	134–160
Coda	C major	160–198

not only because of their contrasting keys, but also because there are many leaps throughout the first one whereas much of the second theme is **conjunct** – that is, it moves by step like a scale:

Haydn is famous for melodies that are either actual quotations of folk music or which sound like folk tunes from the area of Eastern Europe in which he worked. He was particularly fond of melodies that feature the unusual intervals which occur in what is known as the 'gypsy scale', shown *right*. It is the same as the harmonic minor scale except that the fourth degree is sharpened (F♯ in this case) and it thus contains two eastern-sounding intervals of an augmented 2nd. These intervals (marked '*a2*') and the equally characteristic diminished 4th ('*d4*') are a prominent feature of Haydn's C-minor melody and further differentiate it from theme 2.

Yet the two themes are related. In the music example *above* they are aligned to show their similar openings, including the unusual sharpened fourth degree of the scale. Also notice how the first four-bar phrase of each melody moves to the dominant (G) while the second modulates to a perfect cadence in a related key.

Both themes have a contrasting middle section (bar 8 in the first theme, bar 34 in the second) followed by a return to the opening phrase, which occurs in the bass in the case of theme 1. In both themes this repeat is modified after four bars so that the melody remains in the tonic key instead of modulating as it did before.

Because both of these sections fall into two unequal parts defined by repeats and keys they are said to be in **binary** (two-part) form. Because they are each rounded off by a modified repeat of their first parts they are said to be in **rounded binary** form (ABA^1).

Ternary form (ABA), often used in songs, looks similar to rounded binary form but it has a self-contained and contrasting middle section. The repeat signs help make it clear that Haydn's themes are in binary form.

Listening guide

The movement starts with a gaunt **two-part texture** of unison violins supported by cellos doubled at the octave above by violas and at the octave below by double basses. The low C in the bass part is written for the five-string double bass that was still common at this time. Modern bass players need either an extension to their low E string, or a five-string bass, to reach this far down.

Theme 1
Bars 1–26

From bar 8 the melody is retained in the first violins, but it is accompanied by **homophonic** lower strings that increase the texture to three, sometimes four parts. These extra notes are needed fully to realise the expressive **appoggiaturas** at the beginning of most bars. When the first bars of the movement return in bar 16 the two-part string texture also returns, but the melody is initially in the bass with a new violin countermelody above it. The altered melody then passes to the violas (bar 21) and finally back to the violins (bars 22–26).

Homophonic describes a texture in which one part has the melody and the other parts accompany.

An **appoggiatura** is a dissonant note (that is one which is not part of the current chord). The momentary tension created by this effect is released when the appoggiatura resolves to a harmony note. See the example at the foot of page 29.

Theme 2
Bars 26–50

A **pedal** (or 'pedal point') is a sustained or repeated note against which changing harmonies are heard.

With the change of key from C minor to C major comes a new texture in which the first oboe states theme 2, its tone given greater depth by being doubled at the octave below by first violins. Other parts accompany, mainly in parallel 3rds and 6ths, above a tonic **pedal** played by cellos and basses. Notice how unison bassoons are used to strengthen the violas for the cadence in bars 29–30 with witty mid-range staccato notes. In bars 30 and 34 the trills are marked *sf* (an abbreviation of the Italian *sforzando*) to show that there should be a stronger attack at the start of this ornament.

At the beginning of the B section of theme 2 (bar 34^2) Haydn uses this *sforzando*-trill motif in a series of exchanges between different orchestral groupings, with low strings and bassoon being imitated by high strings and oboe. This effect of one group responding to another is known as **antiphony**, and would have had a splendidly stereophonic effect in Haydn's time, when it was usual for the first and second violins to be on opposite sides of the orchestra. The simple harmony of these four bars (chords V^7 and I) is underpinned by another pedal, this time on the dominant note, G.

There are more changes of texture to enchant the listener in this short passage – it should be no surprise that the *Morning Chronicle* reported that the delighted audience encored this slow movement at its first performance. First comes a delicate homophonic passage (bars 39–40), then an expressive phrase for violin and oboe, answered by second violins in bar 42, which links into the return of the theme 2 melody, starting on the last quaver of bar 42.

Haydn now remains in the tonic by transposing the music up a 4th from bar 47 and altering the end to cadence quietly in C. Notice that on the last quaver of bar 49 the second horn doesn't play B, like the second oboe and second violins. This is because the natural horn has only a limited selection of notes available in the lower part of its range (see page 31), and Haydn therefore assigns it G instead. The resulting pattern of a 5th sandwiched between a 3rd and a 6th is shown *left* (remember that horns in C sound an octave lower than written when using the treble clef). This is one of the most characteristic sounds of classical orchestral music and, despite there being only one interval of a 5th involved and despite the fact that trumpets and other instruments are often given a similar pattern, it is known as **horn 5ths**.

Horns in C
(sounding pitch)

'Horn 5ths'

Variation 1
Bars 50–108

This written-out repeat in the first section is the reason why the variation appears to have more bars than the original theme.

In bars 50–58 the only variation is the addition of an oboe countermelody. However, Haydn doesn't merely repeat this phrase as he did at the start, but instead writes out the repeat in full (bars 58–66) in order to rescore this countermelody by adding a flute an octave above the oboe and an answering part for bassoons in octaves. Notice the felicitous touch of the rising bassoon arpeggio in dotted rhythm (bar 66) to carry the music forward across the phrase break.

In the B section the original string parts are maintained but are embellished by a flute countermelody derived from the dotted-rhythm figure of bar 54. When the A section returns at the end of bar 74 it has moved up from the bass (where it was in bar 16^2) to the middle of the texture, where Haydn introduces the new colour combination of a solo bassoon in unison with violas, freeing up the cellos and basses to add gruff low trills in bars 75 and 77.

In the variation of theme 2 (bars 84–108) Haydn introduces a solo violin part for the leader of the orchestra. This ornate triplet version of the original melody is offset by a simple chordal accompaniment played by the rest of the first violins (the **ripieno**) and the other strings. In bars 92–96 the original melody of bars 34–38 disappears altogether and is replaced by sustained wind and detached string chords. However, Haydn retains the basic harmonic progression of his original tune, including the pedals, the modulation to G major and the final perfect cadence (bars 107–108), now embellished with the soloist's **double stopping** over delicate pizzicato (plucked) string chords. Notice that when the horns sustain the pedal in bars 101–106 they are notated in the bass clef. Rather confusingly, the convention in old scores is that horns in C sound an octave *higher* than written when using the bass clef.

Double-stopping is the act of playing a two-note chord on a string instrument by sounding notes on two adjacent strings simultaneously.

This variation opens with a **tutti**, meaning 'all'. The entry of trumpets and drums along with the loud dynamics provides a strong contrast with the delicate textures of the previous variation. The direction 'arco' indicates that the strings should return to bowing. There are three components to the texture of the first four bars:

1. the original melody played in octaves by violins doubled by flutes and oboes
2. a new cello/bass part (doubled by bassoons and partially by violas) that forms a semiquaver counterpoint to the melody
3. brass fanfares on the tonic and dominant reinforced by timpani.

Variation 2
Bars 108–160

At the end of bar 112 the texture dramatically reduces to two parts with *piano* imitations of the dotted figure in bars 114–116.

To vary the B section of theme 1 Haydn first replaces its melody with loud demi-semiquaver scales (bars 117–118). There is another vivid contrast in dynamic at bar 119, and the tune now reappears, but it is broken-up by rests that intensify the effect of the sighing semitones over diminished 7th chords. In the next loud passage (bars 124^2–128) the texture of the first tutti is turned inside out. The theme is held by bass instruments with first violins providing a countermelody. The tonic and dominant brass fanfares are now doubled by flutes and oboes, while the second violins provide a harmonic filling. Similarly contrasting instrumental textures are heard in the last six bars of this section.

For the variation of theme 2 starting at bar 135, Haydn returns to C major and the new sound of a wind ensemble, punctuated by soft pizzicato string chords. For the first time the melody is heard on the first oboe without any doubling. Bassoons articulate the pedal with semiquavers in a bubbling octave pattern while flutes decorate the harmony with sparkling broken chords.

The B section (bars 142^2–160) begins with a more heavily-scored version of bars 34^2–38, answered by four bars in which the original melody of bars 39–42 is heard in simplified form on the first oboe and in a decorated form on flutes and violins (see *right*). This simultaneous use of two different versions of the same melody is known as **heterophony**. The return of the A section at bar 150 begins with an exciting tutti in which the original theme is accompanied by a measured trill in the bass and and stately brass chords. After

the pause, wind alone complete the phrase (notice the 'horn 5ths' again) with just timpani providing the V–I bass for the perfect cadence. Haydn uses a descending scale for flute and oboe to lead into a repeat of these last two bars to round-off his second variation.

Coda
Bars 160–198

The Italian word **coda** means a 'tail' and in music it simply refers to a closing section – later we shall see that many of the jazz works you will study also end with a coda.

Haydn bases his coda on material from the second theme and so it is centred on that theme's C major tonality. In bar 160 the last chord of variation 2 overlaps with a tonic pedal that underpins the first 11 bars of the coda. Above this Haydn spins a texture that is more **contrapuntal** than any yet heard in the movement. The first violins restate the melody of bars 46^2–48 and two bars later a new timbre of oboe doubled by violas imitates this. Meanwhile the second violins play an independent contrapuntal part that forms suspensions above the viola part. On the last quaver of bar 164 the cellos start another imitative entry, leaving the pedal to the double basses, and the first violins take over the suspensions.

A **contrapuntal** texture is one in which two or more parts have simultaneous melodic interest. It is the opposite of a homophonic texture in which there is only one principal tune supported by an accompaniment.

This entire texture tantalisingly collapses as suddenly as it began. At bar 167 Haydn snips his material down to just three notes and repeats this fragment in a very quiet falling sequence. When the fragment is heard again (bars 172–3) it forms a rising sequence far above the semiquaver string chords but by now the audience is thinking that the slow movement is quietly drifting into oblivion, and Haydn is thinking it is time for one of those gestures 'that will make the ladies scream' (as he said of his 'surprise' symphony) and that inevitably helped generate the huge round of applause in London at the end of his slow movements.

And so at bar 174 Haydn plunges *fortissimo* onto what by now seems to be the very remote chord of E♭ major. It is in first inversion, so G is in the bass and this is the only note it has in common with the chord and prevailing key of C major. It is a clever play on the ear – E♭ is the main key of the rest of the symphony – but after so much C major it has the disorientating effect that Haydn so carefully calculated. He reinforces this by settling in E♭ for the next eight bars as a solo oboe and flute play the three-note dotted figure over a minimal broken-chord accompaniment provided by the violins.

The three-note figure is doubled in thirds and rises sequentially in bars 182–6 as the music modulates back to C major and a resplendent recapitulation of bars 42^2–50. The tonic pedal is extended to six bars and is assigned to a platform-shuddering combination – timpani on a repeated C and cellos/basses playing a measured C–B trill. The final perfect cadences (bars 196–8) form the loudest passage in the movement, with all the instruments for the first time marked *ff* and with strings playing double or triple-stopped chords.

In bars 196–8 it is especially important to remember that the double bass sounds an octave lower than written. The lowest note of the final chord, for example, is not the G played by the cellos but C, a 5th lower, sounded by the double basses.

 Private study

1. What is meant by the 'gypsy scale' and what is its relevance to this movement?

2. How many times does Haydn use (a) an augmented 2nd and (b) a diminished 4th in the **first 16 bars** of his theme?

3. Haydn uses two themes in this movement, both in ABA[1] form. Why is this not described as ternary form?
4. How are the two themes related in key and in melodic material?
5. What is meant by the terms appoggiatura and 'horn 5ths'?
6. Explain the difference between the following three textures: homophonic, heterophonic and polyphonic (or contrapuntal).
7. Which instruments did Haydn use in the rest of the *Drumroll* symphony but not in the slow movement?

Composing

There are a number of ideas in this movement that could serve as models for your own compositions, especially Haydn's use of contrasted textures. Variation form is a good way to structure a piece and a double theme, using two contrasted keys, should provide more tonal variety than using just a single theme.

Further reading

Haydn Symphonies by H. C. Robbins Landon. *BBC Consumer Publishing (Books)*, 1966, 1986. ISBN: 0-563-20515-6. This handy BBC Music Guide sometimes goes out of print but it can be found in many libraries and second-hand bookshops.

More detailed books by the same author include **Haydn in England 1791–1795**, *Thames and Hudson*, 1995, ISBN: 0-500-01164-8 and **Essays on the Viennese Classical Style,** *Barrie and Rockliff,* 1970, ISBN 0-214-66794-4.

Selected discography

Philharmonia Hungarica conducted by Antál Dorati. *Decca 452 256-2* (set of two CDs). This double CD is exceptionally good value and includes five other London symphonies. The recordings date from the early 1970s and have attracted consistently good reviews.

London Philharmonic Orchestra conducted by Eugen Jochum. *Deutsche Grammophon 437201-2*. A more expensive four-CD set which includes all of the London symphonies.

Look out for the release of this symphony in the series of highly praised recordings on the *Hyperion* label made by the period instruments of the **Hanover Band**, conducted by Roy Goodman.

Question practice

1. Briefly describe some of the different orchestral textures used by Haydn in this movement.
2. What features of Haydn's music do you think made it so popular?
3. To what extent were composers limited by the brass instruments available in the late 18th century?
4. Briefly comment on the types of variation technique used by Haydn in this movement.

Answer the following question only after you have also studied *West End Blues*.

5. The slow movement of Haydn's Symphony No 103 and Louis Armstrong's *West End Blues* are both centred on a single key. Explain how both pieces achieve variety despite this limitation.

Prescribed for examination in 2003 and 2004 **Piano Concerto in A (first movement)** **Mozart**

A concerto is a large-scale composition for contrasting musical forces, most commonly a soloist (or group of soloists) and an orchestra. The basic design of three movements in a fast–slow–fast pattern was established in the early 18th century, and was widely used by late baroque composers such as Bach. The violin was the most popular choice of solo instrument at that time and Vivaldi's set of four violin concertos called *The Four Seasons* are probably the best-known examples from that period.

The pianoforte

The name *pianoforte* (literally 'soft-loud'), which we now abbreviate to piano, drew attention to the most revolutionary feature of this new instrument – the capability to shape the dynamic of every note. Keyboard instruments such as the harpsichord and organ cannot do this.

In the late 18th century the pianoforte or fortepiano (the terms were used interchangeably at the time) took over from the harpsichord as the principal keyboard instrument of the day. Although early pianos were lighter in tone than modern instruments, they offered a more sustained sound than the harpsichord and allowed direct dynamic control over every note. Bach's youngest son, J. C. Bach, did much to promote the popularity of the new instrument in London, particularly with his publication of six concertos in 1763. They were published as suitable for piano or harpsichord – descriptions of this sort, or the generic German term *Klavier* (keyboard) proving to be a useful way of maximising the piano-music market for some years to come. J. C. Bach's work had a considerable influence on the young Mozart, who met him on an extended visit to England in 1764–5.

The classical concerto

The piano soon proved to be an ideal choice as the solo instrument in a concerto because:

- it could balance with the sound of the larger orchestras of the day more effectively than the harpsichord
- it could provide its own accompaniment and thus take the spotlight with minimal orchestral distraction
- its agility and subtlety of colour provided composer-performers such as Mozart with a showcase to display their virtuosity.

During the classical period concertos, like symphonies, started being played in public concert halls to large audiences. As a result, and particularly in Mozart's later works, the concerto grew longer and the role of the soloist became more prominent.

First movement form

The first movement begins with the orchestra preparing for the entry of the soloist by introducing some of the main themes in the tonic key. There is then usually a solo version of the main theme, a modulation to the dominant and often some new solo material in this key. The orchestra concludes this first section (the **exposition**) with a partial return (a **ritornello** or 'little return') of the opening material, this time in the dominant key. The use of two related key centres for substantial sections of the exposition is also a feature of 'sonata form' used in the sonatas and symphonies of this period and is something we shall encounter in some of the other set works.

In a minor-key movement the two principal key centres are often the tonic and relative major, rather than tonic and dominant.

The second main section for the soloist creates tension through the use of wider ranging and more rapid changes of key, like the middle section (**development**) of a sonata form movement. Often there is indeed development of earlier themes and sometimes, as in this movement, the introduction of new material.

Warning. Photocopying any part of this book without permission is illegal.

The final section, or **recapitulation**, resolves this tension by presenting the material of the exposition in the tonic key, although some cuts and changes of order may be employed. Almost always there is the opportunity for the soloist to perform a **cadenza**, an improvised display of virtuosity, before a final *tutti* brings the movement to a close.

Form	Main keys	Bars
Exposition	A/E major	1–142
Development	various	143–197
Recapitulation	A major	198–314

Almost all music written before 1800 was composed for a specific purpose, such as a concert, publication or commission. Mozart finished K488 on 2 March 1786, ready to perform on 7 April during the annual season of concerts he had inaugurated in Vienna. He had moved there some five years earlier to establish a career free of the ties of aristocratic employment that supported most composers at the time. Establishing a reputation in order to attract wealthy pupils and commissions for new works was therefore of paramount importance to Mozart, and the public performance of his own concertos was an essential part of that process. Despite his efforts the audiences in Vienna were fickle in their tastes and although Mozart had enjoyed some initial success it is noteworthy that he gave only the one concert in that season's programme.

You will often see Mozart's works identified as K followed by a number, such as K488. The letter refers to Köchel, an Austrian who catalogued Mozart's surviving music in the 19th-century. The numbering system helps to differentiate works that have identical titles, such as the two piano concertos in A, K414 and K488.

Most of Mozart's concertos are scored for a relatively small orchestra. In K488 he uses only one flute and omits the penetrating sound of two oboes in preference for the mellifluous timbre of clarinets, instruments that Mozart was starting to use increasingly often at the time and which suit the lyricism of this concerto. However they were still sufficiently novel for him to write to a patron:

Instrumentation

> There are two clarinets in the A-major concerto. Should His Highness not have clarinets at his court … the first [clarinet] part should be played by a violin and the second by a viola.

Two bassoons and two horns complete the wind section. Remember that clarinets in A and horns in A both sound a minor 3rd lower than written. Strings are in the usual four parts with basses mainly playing the same notes as cellos but sounding an octave lower.

Listening guide

The work begins with an eight-bar phrase for strings (ending on the dominant) answered by eight bars for wind, an octave higher, ending on the tonic. This structure of balanced phrases in which an 'antecedent' is followed by a 'consequent' is a feature of the Viennese classical style and such balance is known as **periodic phrasing**. Mozart cleverly avoids the predictability this can generate by repeating the cadence of bars 15–16, with some added decoration, and then overlapping the end of this second cadence by starting the next phrase in bar 18.

Orchestral exposition
Bars 1–66

These opening 17 bars contain other features which make the classical style so recognisable, such as the clear melodic line based on chord and scale patterns, the mainly chordal accompaniment with minimal counterpoint, and the use of simple, 'functional' harmonies which, with the help of a short tonic pedal and regular cadence points, define the tonic key of A major.

Mozart's scoring for the first real *tutti* at bar 18 is subtle. The melody is high in the flute, where it can be heard above the ensemble, and instead of merely doubling it with violins an octave lower Mozart

Warning. Photocopying any part of this book without permission is illegal.

alternates between octave and unison doubling. In bars 23–26 the simple flute melody is accompanied by a more elaborate version of the same tune played by violins (an effect known as **heterophony**). In bars 28–29 a dominant pedal and wind fanfares bring this first section to a close on the dominant.

At the upbeat to bar 31 the texture reduces to three parts and the dynamic to *piano* a second subject based on repeated notes and a falling scale. When the phrase begins to repeat (bar 38) Mozart doubles the violin melody an octave lower on the first bassoon then adds adds the flute an octave above the violins. Flutes and bassoons playing melodies two octaves apart are one of the most typical and felicitous instrumental effects to be found in Mozart's wind scoring.

A pedal note on A returns in bar 46, but it now supports a briefly dark passage of D minor harmony in which first violins are echoed by woodwind while inner parts play a semiquaver filling (indicated by crotchets with two slashes through the stems).

D minor becomes D major but the expected cadence in the tonic at bars 51–52 is interrupted and Mozart briefly explores the relative minor key (F♯ minor) with another new motif in the woodwind (bar 52) which the first violins invert in reply. A chromatic scale and crescendo lead to a busy violin line with syncopated accompaniment from the wind. The melody moves to solo woodwind in octaves with the drop in dynamic at bar 62 for the **codetta** (a short concluding section). This has the dual function of reasserting the tonic key (notice the frequent use of chords I and V) and of preparing the audience for *the* event – the entry of the soloist.

Solo exposition
Bars 67–136

The **Alberti bass** is named after an Italian composer who was rather addicted to the idea of sounding the notes of a chord in the order low, high, middle and high again.

The solo piano enters gently, with the first subject in the right hand and an **Alberti bass** in the left. As a light string accompaniment commences (bar 71) the piano begins to elaborate this theme, the scale-based figuration becoming more continuous and impressive during the repeat. When the *tutti* enters in bar 82 Mozart is still essentially repeating the opening music but after 23 bars (at bar 87) he starts to guide the music towards the dominant key of E major. The non-thematic piano figuration (often blandly described as 'passagework') elaborates the harmonies in the accompaniment and gives the soloist a showcase for an extended display of virtuosity.

By bar 98 Mozart has so convicingly established the dominant as the new focus of attention that he is able to come to rest on a chord of B major ('the dominant of the dominant') thus preparing the way for the unaccompanied piano to restate the second subject, heard originally in A major at bar 31 but now in E major at bar 99. Again the piano decorates the repeat of the theme at bar 107, this time with glittering broken octaves. This passage shows the opposite poles of the pianist's role in the concerto. In the first phrase the soloist alone is the centre of attention, in the second the piano adds touches of brilliance to the music played by solo wind and first violins.

The melody returns to the piano at bar 114, with the left hand playing a decorated version of the horn pedal. Compare this with bar 46 (and bar 120 with bar 52) to see how Mozart is not just transposing the opening music but decorating and re-orchestrating it as well. From bar 124 Mozart diverges more markedly from this material. Instead of the busy string writing that we had earlier the spotlight is now on the soloist's virtuoso figuration. However much of the original harmonic scheme is still present and is outlined by the left-hand chords and the string and wind accompaniment.

The technique of finishing the solo exposition with a passage of solo *bravura*, a cadential 6–4 (bar 135) and a long trill (bar 136) is one of Mozart's favourite ways to herald the arrival of the ritornello. Notice how the final chord of the cadence in bar 137 seamlessly overlaps with the start of this ritornello in the dominant. This begins with a transposed version of the opening material, starting from bar 18. However after some semiquaver scales Mozart suddenly stops in mid-phrase, emphasising the deliberate hiatus with a silence in the first half of bar 143. This was a very 'little return' indeed!

The Italian word *bravura* means 'courage' or 'swagger' and refers to a brilliant display of performing technique.

The silence in bar 143 introduces a new texture of suspensions played by closely-spaced strings (while cellos are often above violas in this passage, remember that double basses sound an octave lower than written and thus provide the real bass to the chords). It also introduces yet another theme in a movement already overflowing with melodic ideas. Mozart's purpose, in this unusual turn of events, is to bring back the soloist as quickly as possible, without making the audience wait through a long ritornello. This happens in bar 149, where the piano starts to decorate the new 'development theme' in delicate two-part counterpoint, the high texture contrasting strongly with the rich, low strings.

Development Bars 143–197

In bar 156 unaccompanied wind use the first two bars of the new theme to plunge from E major to E minor. This is answered by staccato strings, doubled and decorated by piano. These textures alternate in antiphonal exchanges as the tonality becomes much more turbulent with modulating sequences that rapidly dive down in thirds from E minor through C major (bar 162), A minor (166), F major (168) and D minor (170). Such rapidly changing tonal centres are an important feature of development sections and will later be resolved by a substantial recapitulation in the tonic.

At bar 170 Mozart begins the most complex instrumental texture in the movement. The main melodic line is played by the first clarinet, imitated by the flute one bar later, the two parts forming a free canon (free because the first interval played on the flute does not *exactly* replicate the first interval played on the clarinet). It is based on the first clarinet part of bars 156–158, which in turn Mozart derived from the development theme itself (see *right*). The most significant development is the opening leap, added in bar 156 where it was a 4th, but now augmented (enlarged) to an expressive upward tenth. Below this the piano right-hand drives the music on in continuous semiquavers, while the left-hand and bassoon supply the bass (the bassoon ingeniously reflecting the clarinet's upward tenths with its own descending tenths). This complex pattern is repeated twice in descending sequence (bars 172 and 174).

Mozart begins to prepare for the return of the tonic key from bar 178 by sounding or implying the dominant in each of the next 20 bars, mainly as a pedal point in cellos and basses or horns. Above the pedal strikingly dissonant harmonies resolve towards chords Ic and V, but the tonic is still minor at this stage. The dissonances arise from yet another variant of the development theme in which the opening interval now becomes a semitone, the F♮ creating a deeply expressive minor 9th with the bass E (see *left*). The same type of astringent harmony is formed when imitative woodwinds answer the strings two bars later. These four bars are then repeated. The piano continues to embellish the orchestral parts, but from bar 186 it becomes the main focus of attention and the harmony homes in yet closer towards the tonic with a long V^7 in bars 194–7.

Recapitulation Bars 198–314

The long-expected tonic key arrives with the return of the opening material in bar 198. We now see another reason why Mozart abbreviated the earlier ritornello. The development was entirely concerned with exploring its own special theme and this means that the many various tunes of the exposition can now return after their long absence, sounding as fresh and welcome as the tonic key itself, despite the length of this section.

The recapitulation is not merely a restatement of the exposition. The piano plays an integral role in this recapitulation resulting in many changes of scoring and figuration. Mozart snips two bars to bring in bar 213 earlier than expected, but later adds three extra bars (225–227). Bar 258 corresponds with bar 60 but next he jumps straight to material from bar 141, allowing the return of the development theme in the tonic, delightfully rescored for clarinets and bassoons on its repeat in bars 267–275. Mozart then resumes the use of music transposed from the exposition. Bars 282–3 contain the cadential 6–4 and climactic trill, followed by the short (and still interrupted) ritornello but this time the following appearance of the development theme is tantalising short. The orchestra judders to a halt in bar 297 on a second inversion of A, and then waits for the soloist's cadenza. This ends with the marked V^7 and trill, and the orchestra rounds off the movement with material that had not been heard since its original appearance in bars 49–66. Mozart concisely snips eight bars (52–58) from this repeat and adds four additional *tutti* bars at the end.

Private study

1. What do the terms ritornello and appoggiatura mean?

2. Look at bars 9 and 10. Does the first clarinet play (i) the same notes as the flute, (ii) the same notes as the flute but a 6th lower, (iii) the same notes as the flute but an octave lower?

3. Explain the following indications: 'tutti' (bar 1), '1.' (bassoons, bar 15), 'a2' (bassoons, bars 18–19), 'cadenza' (bar 298).

4. Read the explanation of 'horn 5ths' on page 34 and then state where Mozart uses horn 5ths in this movement.

5. Make an outline comparison of the exposition and recapitulation, showing how Mozart adapts his material when it returns in the recapitulation. This could be written out as a table.

Warning. Photocopying any part of this book without permission is illegal.

Groupwork

Listen carefully to the piano cadenza in your recording. Can you identify in detail how it relates to the rest of the movement and the improvising techniques used by the pianist? Try to notate some of the music, even if only as a rough sketch.

Composing

Write your own cadenza for this movement. If you are not a pianist you could sketch the main melodic ideas and harmonies, and then work with a pianist to develop some idiomatic piano figuration.

Look in detail at Mozart's woodwind writing and note the many different textures he creates despite the relatively limited resources used. Can you make use of any of these ideas? For example, experiment with a clarinet part that doubles the flute (i) in unison, (ii) an octave lower, (iii) two octaves lower. Be sure to work out the transposition correctly otherwise you will hear some odd (but perhaps useful!) results.

Further reading

A Companion to Mozart's Piano Concertos by Arthur Hutchings. *Clarendon Press*, 1998. ISBN: 0-19-816708-3.

The Cambridge Companion to the Piano by David Rowland. *Cambridge University Press*, 1998. ISBN: 0-521-47986-X. This deals with the history and repertoire of the piano (including its use in jazz).

Selected discography

Murray Perahia with the English Chamber Orchestra. *Sony SK 39064*. Directed from the keyboard by the soloist, this CD also includes Mozart's piano concerto in F, K459.

Mitsuko Uchida with the English Chamber Orchestra conducted by Jeffrey Tate. *Philips 420187-2*. K482 is on the same CD. Also look out for recordings by Barenboim, Kempff, Brendel and Ashkenazy.

Malcolm Bilson with the English Baroque Soloists conducted by John Eliot Gardiner. *Deutsche Grammophon 447295-2*. Also look out for the recording by Robert Levin (*L'Oiseau Lyre 452052-2*). Both use a fortepiano and an orchestra of period instruments.

Question practice

1. Outline some of the ways in which the piano relates to the orchestra in this movement.
2. Comment on Mozart's writing for wind instruments in this movement.
3. In what ways did the sound of the piano in Mozart's day differ from the sound of the modern piano?
4. The word virtuosity refers to exceptional technical skill. To what extent do you feel that Mozart's concerto requires virtuosity from the soloist?

Answer the following questions only after you have studied at least some of the prescribed jazz works.

5. How does the role of the soloist in Mozart's concerto differ from the role of a soloist in jazz?
6. Compare the type of improvisation needed in a classical cadenza with the type of improvisation used by jazz musicians. What are the main differences in approach?

Symphony No 5 (fourth movement)   Beethoven

Beethoven's roots were as much in the Viennese classical style as Mozart and Haydn, but he was of a later generation (born in 1770) and of a very different disposition. For Beethoven, composing was a long process of noting and polishing musical ideas, sketching and revising, changing and refining. This is quite the opposite of the swift, skilled craft of his 18th-century predecessors and the result is immediately apparent in a simple count of their symphonies – some 108 by Haydn, 41 by Mozart and nine by Beethoven.

Beethoven used the musical language of classical music but he considerably extended its vocabulary, particularly in the use of:

- wider ranging modulations, especially to keys that are a 3rd away from the tonic
- dissonant chords employed for their dramatic effect
- terse, rhythmic motifs, capable of infinite transformation
- longer movements that develop over a broad time-scale
- larger orchestras, in which not only is the double-wind section the norm, but additional instruments such as trombones, piccolo and contrabassoon are sometimes used – and in which the number of string players has to be increased to balance.

Each of Beethoven's nine symphonies is highly individual, often seeming to explore different aspects of a profound philosophical truth across all four movements, as we shall see in this symphony. Most are longer than their 18th-century predecessors – his third symphony extends the full symphonic experience to 50 minutes. In his first movements greater length arises from longer development sections and, to balance this, the extension of the coda into a full section in its own right. The middle two movements are often substantial and strongly characterised. For example in his third symphony (the *Eroica*, or 'heroic') instead of a song-like *andante* there is a funeral march of gigantic proportions, and for the triple-time movement he wrote an ultra-fast scherzo that is overflowing with animal high spirits instead of the traditional courtly minuet. Finally, instead of concluding with the type of jolly rondo so beloved of Haydn, Beethoven usually prefers a large and impressive finale which balances and resolves the philosophical struggles and musical debates that have gone before.

In the 18th century almost all the music played at concerts was contemporary. New pieces quickly went out of fashion and composers such as Bach and Vivaldi were forgotten after their deaths until their music was rediscovered much later. Most of Beethoven's works, on the other hand, continued to be played after his death in 1827 and had a profound influence on 19th-century music. Beethoven was probably the first composer to realise that his music would live on beyond him. In a remarkable document of 1802 he wrote how the knowledge of his oncoming and incurable deafness had driven him to thoughts of suicide but, revealing a sense of his own destiny, he adds:

> It was art alone that held me back, for it seemed to me to be impossible to leave the world until I had created all that I felt destined to give to the world.

Composition

Beethoven wrote his fifth symphony in 1807–8, although some of the initial ideas were conceived several years earlier. It was given its first performance on 22 Dec 1808 at the *Theater an der Wien* in Vienna, in a concert of prodigious length and typical diversity for the period – it also included his new sixth symphony, a piano concerto, a new choral work (which broke down in performance and had to be restarted), excerpts from opera and church music, and Beethoven himself improvising at the piano. All of this occupied the audience for four hours in a freezing theatre. The first performance of perhaps the most famous symphony in the world was not an outstanding success!

To make sense of the last movement it is essential to listen to the entire symphony, to which the finale is not only joined by a musical link but is also the triumphant, major-key climax. The extra-musical meaning of the first movement could not be clearer; Beethoven himself said of the initial four-note motive 'Thus fate knocks at the door'. The emotional weight of this movement falls on its volcanic coda. Instead of a feeling of closure its mighty C-minor cadences leave the listener shell shocked, searching for some resolution of the tensions generated by Beethoven's mortal combat with fate. What follows in the slow movement is not resolution, but consolation (in the lyrical A♭ major theme) and renewed tension (in the blaring C-major fanfares that invade the lyricism). The *Allegro* that forms the third movement is in the form of a *scherzo* – a fast triple-time movement. The word *scherzo* means a 'joke' although this is a pretty grim joke, for this is music which returns to C minor and alternates between ghostly, questioning phrases and loud, despairing outbursts.

It is at the end of this third movement that Beethoven completely breaks with classical precedent. Instead of a coda, an interrupted cadence (bars 323–324) leads to a passage where all movement is suspended save for the softest tapping on a kettledrum. When the first theme returns (bars 339–341) it is distorted into an even more ghostly form. Cellos and basses add a pulsing G to the timpani's C from bar 350, forming a double pedal. As the violins rise out of the abyss, the fragments of the main theme begin to hint at the major key and then, with a colossal crescendo, break free into the light of C major at the start of the finale.

This is the resolution of the titanic struggles of the first movement and the victory over what novelist E. M. Forster called the 'goblins' of the third movement. But Beethoven had fought his own demons for long enough to know that they could return. 'Look out for the part where you think you have done with the goblins and they come back' says Helen Schlegel in Forster's *Howard's End*. The passage to which she refers is the return of the ghostly tapping in bars 153–206 of the last movement. Miraculously this passage fulfils several functions simultaneously. It is a reminder of the malignancy of fate. Its minor mode makes the diatonic C-major tonality of the following recapitulation shine more brightly. It binds two movements of the symphony together in a way no previous composer had attempted. Finally it acts as a passage of dominant preparation that creates tension which is released with the first long-awaited major triad at the start of the recapitulation.

Warning. Photocopying any part of this book without permission is illegal.

return like a flash-back – yet it is not in our imagination, for the music is real and the glorious C-major party has indeed been interrupted by this visitation from the past. Beethoven's brilliant calculation of the psychological effect of this moment has received much comment over the last two centuries. There is no real context for this summoning-up of a dark mood that had already been dispelled and there is no development of the material it recalls. In the words of the commentator Donald Tovey,

> Beethoven recalls the third movement as a memory we know for a fact but can no longer understand ... the depth and the darkness are alike absent, and in the dry light of day we cannot remember our fears of the unknown.

Bars 183–206 use nothing but dominant harmony, underpinned in the last four bars by a tonic pedal. A quick crescendo reminds us of where we were, the darkness has passed and Beethoven embarks on the recapitulation.

Recapitulation
Bars 207–294

From a formal point of view the recapitulation is so regular that it requires little comment. The first subject (bars 207–232) is repeated note-for-note. The transition is modified from bar 238 where a touch of chromaticism ensures that it remains in the tonic key of C major instead of modulating to the dominant as it did in the exposition. The second subject (bars 253–294) is an almost exact repeat of bars 44–76, but new, grinding discords in bars 285–293 increase tension to fever pitch and lead directly to the coda.

Coda
Bars 294–444

At 150 bars this is the longest section of the movement, yet it never leaves the home key of C major (non-diatonic notes are either melodic decorations or notes of chromatic chords that simply add colour to what are otherwise diatonic harmonic progressions). The goblins really are banished forever by this joyous, life-affirming review of the principal thematic ideas of the finale. Bars 294–307 are based on motifs x and y, with the triplets becoming continuous in the last five bars. Perfect cadences in bars 313–6 seem to signal the end, but a new version of the transition theme is developed from bar 317. Bars 334–349 are a rescored version of bars 317–332.

An *accelerando* in bars 353–361 leads to the *Presto* (one beat per bar) in which the second theme of the second subject is repeatedly played at something approaching three times its original speed. From bar 390 the opening bars of the finale are given similar treatment and the symphony ends with numerous perfect cadences followed by 29 bars of C-major tonic chords in countless spacings, rising for one last time through the initial tonic triad of the opening motif in bars 428–432.

Private study

1. In what ways did Beethoven extend the language of classical music?

2. Why does the opening of the last movement of this symphony make such an impact?

3. What are the three main parts of sonata form called?

4. What distinguishes the middle of these three sections from the outer two?

5. Name the instruments used by Beethoven in this movement that were not normally found in symphonies at this time. What do these instruments contribute to the total effect?

6. Define the terms 'diatonic' and 'homophonic' and give the bar numbers of passages to which each of these terms might apply.

7. In which bar(s) does the orchestra play descending scales in octaves?

8. In which part of the movement does Beethoven use counterpoint to create tension?

9. Explain why only the top note of the chord in the first violin part of bar 6 is shown as a minim.

Composing

Explore the techniques Beethoven uses to build-up tension at the end of the development. In particular look at the precise chords he uses over the dominant pedal which starts at bar 132, noting how they become increasingly chromatic and dissonant.

Further reading

Beethoven Symphonies by Robert Simpson. *BBC Consumer Publishing (Books)*, 1970, 1986. ISBN: 0-563-20484-2. A short and very reasonably priced introduction.

The Nine Symphonies of Beethoven by Antony Hopkins. *Scolar Press*, 1996. ISBN: 1-85928-246-6.

Selected discography

Vienna Philharmonic Orchestra conducted by Carlos Kleiber. *Deutsche Grammophon 447400-2*. Many regard this legendary mid-1970s recording as the most exhilarating of all the dozens of currently available recordings – Beethoven's seventh symphony is on the same CD. Other highly respected recordings include those by Otto Klemperer with the Philharmonia Orchestra and Herbert von Karajan with the Berlin Philharmonic Orchestra.

Orchestre révolutionnaire et romantique conducted by John Eliot Gardiner. *Deutsche Grammophon 447 062-2*. This is one of several recent recordings on period instruments. Beethoven's sixth symphony is on the same CD.

Question practice

1. What aspects of Beethoven's music were new and forward-looking?

2. This movement requires larger orchestral forces than most symphonic music of the period. Explain how Beethoven uses the additional resources at his disposal.

3. Describe the techniques used by Beethoven to create the enormous orchestral build-up in the passage immediately before the music from the previous movement returns.

4. Comment on the ways in which Beethoven exploited, rather than was restricted by, the natural-brass instruments of his day.

5. Describe how classical composers used relationships between different keys to structure a movement.

Overture to The Barber of Seville — Rossini

Prescribed for examination in 2001

Gioacchino Rossini (1792–1868) cultivated the Italian *opera buffa*, a type of comic opera that reached its zenith in Mozart's *The Marriage of Figaro*. In fact the barber in Rossini's opera is none other than Figaro, the hero of Mozart's earlier work. As a composer of comic operas Rossini was a conservative, interested in enchanting his audiences with simple melodies and clear rhythms. In many respects his style is closer to that of 18th-century composers such as Mozart than to the contemporary romantic style then emerging in Germany.

The *buffo* style is seen at its simplest in the G-major theme that starts in bar 92. It is the main second subject in the sonata-form structure. The melody delights because it is immediately memorable – the sort of tune that one might whistle after the show is over. What makes it memorable is the way it clearly outlines the tonic chord in the first three bars, and the way the simple repeated dotted rhythms on the tonic lead to a seasoning of chromatic colour. To make sure we remember it Rossini immediately repeats it a tone higher: not quite an exact sequence, but sufficiently near for us to feel the question-and-answer (or antecedent and consequent) structure of these balanced four-bar phrases that are so typical of late 18th-century classical styles. The homophonic accompaniment is kept as straightforward as possible so that the impact of the melody should be unencumbered by harmonic or contrapuntal complexity. In fact the entirely diatonic progression simply uses chord I, IV and V^7 with the most obvious perfect cadence at the end. The only icing on the cake is the cheeky semiquaver figure (bars 95 and 99) that wittily mocks the pathetic pretensions of the two chromatic dissonances. As with any good tune there is nothing nicer than hearing it again in a different scoring (bars 104–115).

The Rossini crescendo

At bar 123 Rossini begins a device that became such a finger-print of his style that it has earned itself the title of a 'Rossini crescendo'. This consists of sequences (such as bars 123–124), repeated phrases (compare bars 123–126 with bars 127–130 and 131–134) and repetitions of fragments of phrases (bar 135 is immediately repeated three times). These repetitions are heard over alternating tonic and dominant chords (one of each per bar at the start, speeding up to two per bar in bars 135–138). Meanwhile more and more instruments are added and the dynamic level rises until the climax of bars 147–149 (where the chords change every beat of the bar).

Rossini dispenses with the potential complexities of a development section and writes a simple four-bar modulation so that the first subject can begin again in bar 154 (this type of structure is known as **abridged sonata form**). When he reaches the second subject Rossini puts his themes into E major so they can appear in the tonic without losing their major-key quality. After the long crescendo has raised the roof for a second time Rossini caps it with a coda. This takes the customary form of a 'stretto' in which the beat suddenly becomes faster (più mosso at bar 225), the melody becomes syncopated (229–232), and chromatic chords are introduced (bars 233–5) to help whip up the level of excitement to fever pitch.

In all these ways the passages we have so far discussed are typical of late *opera buffa* style. But why does this overture to a very jolly comic opera have its main theme in a minor key? To answer this question we must relate this overture to its origins.

> Nothing primes inspiration more than necessity, whether it be the presence of a copyist waiting for your work or the prodding of an impresario tearing his hair out. In my time all Italian impresarios went bald before they were thirty ...
>
> I wrote the sinfonia to *The Thieving Magpie* (*La gazza ladra*) on the day of its first performance in the theatre itself ...
>
> I did better with *The Barber*. I did not compose an overture, but chose for it a sinfonia that I had written for a semi-serious opera called *Elizabeth*. The public was completely satisfied.
>
> (Rossini in a letter to an unknown correspondent)

Italian operatic overtures

Rossini's use of the term *sinfonia* as an apparent synonym for overture is significant. In the baroque era the sinfonia played before an opera started was an independent piece, thematically unconnected with the vocal music that followed. As we can see in the above quotation, Rossini was quite content with this traditional concept of a sinfonia being a curtain-raiser unrelated to the opera itself. And this is where a considerable problem arises.

The classical symphony partly developed out of the Italian opera overture, or *sinfonia* – hence the similarity in their names.

Having written *The Barber of Seville* (*Il barbiere di Siviglia*) in record time (some two to three weeks), Rossini had still not written the overture by the opening night, 20 February 1816. He says that he selected the overture to *Elizabeth, Queen of England* (*Elisabetta, regina d'Inghilterra*, 1815), but all the evidence points to him using the sinfonia that he wrote in 1813 for *Aureliano in Palmira*, a serious opera that was scored for smaller forces than *Elizabeth*. The truth of the matter is that Rossini, having as usual missed the deadline of the opening night, took the overture to *Aureliano* and rescored it for *Elizabeth*, adding trombones in the process.

The confusion about the precise source for the overture to *The Barber of Seville* also explains some notable differences between different editions of the score and recordings. These matters are made worse by the performance practices in early 19th-century Italian opera houses. If you have the Dover score of the opera (a republication of an undated Italian score) will see the strange information '2 flutes = 2 piccolos'. Of course they are not the same! The editor is indicating that whatever permutation the orchestra could manage (two flutes, two piccolos or one of each) could be used. The percussion can be just as confusing. It was then the custom to treat the bass drum part as a rough guide to where any available percussion should start up. So, even though Rossini only wrote a part for *gran cassa* (bass drum) the percussionists might supplement its on-the-beat notes with cymbal clashes on every off-beat (the familiar 'boom-tish' rhythm of marching bands).

The Listening guide in this chapter refers to the Ricordi Critical Edition dating from 1969. This is available in a relatively inexpensive miniature score format which also includes five other overtures by Rossini. If you notice any discrepancies between our account and your own score and recording, check them with your teacher and enjoy having some first-hand experience of the sort of problems that face musicologists when dealing with conflicting sources of old music! In the exam, if there should be any doubt, tell the examiner which edition of the score and which recording you have used.

Discrepancies extend to pitches and rhythms. A couple of examples will have to suffice. Firstly, in older scores the flute (or should it be piccolo?) is given a double sharp at the end of bar 4 (likewise in the echo of this figure played by the first violins), yet in most modern recordings an F♯ is played. Secondly, in older scores the

Warning. Photocopying any part of this book without permission is illegal.

cello/bass part of bar 9 is on the beat (making an 'um-cha' rhythm with the violins), but in later editions and some recordings all of the strings (apart from violas) play off the beat, thus creating a lighter, more syncopated accompaniment to the wind melodies.

Instrumentation

Rossini uses the standard double-wind orchestra of the time (see page 30). The clarinets are in C so do not transpose. The horn parts are for natural horns crooked in E (*corni in mi* in Italian) that sound a minor 6th lower than printed, but the players are later required to change crooks to convert their instruments to horns in G (sounding a perfect 4th lower than printed pitch) – in the 1969 Ricordi score this is indicated by the direction *Si preparino in sol* at bar 78. The trumpets are in A (*trombe in la*) and sound a minor third lower than printed. Trombones appear in some scores (see above) but many recordings omit these instruments altogether.

The timpani are tuned to the tonic and dominant (E and B). The only non-pitched percussion is the bass drum but cymbals may be added in some performances, as explained earlier. The *sistro* (a bell tree or jingles) listed in the Dover score does not feature in the overture. In the strings the double basses mainly (not invariably) play the same notes as the cellos but sound an octave lower.

Form	Main keys	Bars
Introduction	E	0–24
Exposition	e and G	25–153
Recapitulation	e and E	154–224
Coda	E	225–264

Listening guide

This movement uses a structure that Rossini adopted for many of his opera overtures, a slow introduction which leads without break into a fast movement in abridged sonata form.

Introduction
Bars 0–24

The introduction is in the tonic key of E major throughout. It begins with a repeated *tutti* chord, a call to attention. This is followed by two motifs, the rising scale figure played in octaves in bar 1 and the dotted-note figure in bar two played by woodwind and immediately echoed by the strings. The whole phrase is then repeated in sequence over dominant harmony. The section ends with an oboe melody over chromatic semiquaver chords which the strings are directed to play *a punta d'arco* (at the top end of the bow) in some scores. This opening section ends with a decisive cadential 6–4 pattern (Ic–V^7–I in bars 9–11).

A middle section begins at bar 11 with a four-bar aria-like melody for violins (later doubled by flute) featuring expressive appoggiaturas at the start of bars 12 and 13. This contrasts with a delicate accompaniment for pizzicato strings which looks complex but is just a decorative version of a simple progression (IV–II–V^7–I in bars 12–13) ending with the expected Ic–V–I cadence.

The last section of this simple ternary structure begins at bar 17 by repeating the opening motif in a new rising sequence that makes reference to the subdominant and dominant keys (V^{7}b–I in A major and B major). This is followed by inversions of the motif (in other words, the ascending scale now descends) set against legato quavers while the horns hold a dominant pedal. The introduction ends on the dominant of E major.

Exposition
Bars 25–153

The tempo is marked fast and lively (essentially two minim beats per bar) and some scores add the word *battute* – strict time. The first subject (bars 25–47) is in the tonic minor and consists of a theme made out of detached fragments of melody, nearly all of them derived from motif *a* (see *right*). The grace notes are played as shown in this example (which also indicates how even shorter motifs are derived from *a*). The texture in the first eight bars is chordal with the melody doubled in octaves by violas (and, in some scores and recordings, doubled at the octave above by a piccolo). The harmony could not be simpler. Chord I is repeated throughout bars 25–31 to be followed by V^7b–I and then an imperfect cadence (IVb–V).

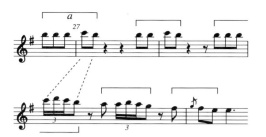

At bar 34 a contrasting texture of woodwind (and violas) in octaves introduces a new figure. This begins with off-beat syncopation and its first note is immediately shortened to allow faster repetitions (bar 33), both devices guaranteed to raise the excitement level.

A repeat begins in bar 39 but now a touch of G major is introduced (bars 44–45). This is purely decorative since the harmony immediately returns to E minor and a perfect cadence in bars 47–48.

The transition to the second subject (bars 48–90) begins with a new idea, a violin arpeggio with brass fanfares, which is presented in antiphonal exchanges with a woodwind quaver figure. This is one of the most complex textures of the whole overture, so the harmony is kept as simple as possible: four bars of chord I and four bars of chord V. A repeat begins in bars 56–59, but this time the underlying chord has a pivotal function. It is not only chord I of E minor but also chord VI of G major (the ultimate destination of the transition) and this leads to a perfect cadence in G at bars 63–64. Bars 64–71 are the most chromatic and contrapuntal of the whole overture, but after chord V of G is reached in bar 72 Rossini concentrates on a lengthy dominant preparation for the second subject, adding colour with chromatic notes (B♭ and E♭) borrowed from the tonic minor (G minor). The texture becomes thinner until just the first violins are left with a descending scale which we expect to land on G as the second subject begins in the relative major. The four bars of trills are a typically Rossinian tease which delays the happy outcome of his comically inflated modulation from E minor to G major.

Most aspects of the second subject have already been discussed on the first page of this chapter. At bar 115 Rossini takes its opening bar, repeats it and then inverts it (bar 117) rounding off the phrase with a chromatic A♯ that picks up the flavour of bars 95 and 99. As expected the phrase is immediately repeated. After the 'Rossini crescendo', and instead of a development, a simple and very brief modulation (bars 150–4) leads directly to the recapitulation.

Recapitulation
Bars 154–224

The first subject in E minor (bars 154–176) is an exact repeat of bars 25–47. Since the second subject material (bars 177–224) is in the tonic major no transition is needed, so all the melodrama of bars 48–90 is simply ditched. Apart from some delightful rescoring (such as bassoon instead of horn in bars 189–197) the rest of this section is just a straight transposition of bars 91–138.

Coda
Bars 225–264

The coda, with its use of a 'stretto' to build excitement, has already been mentioned. Rossini continues to rely on repetition, bars 238–250 being a restatement of bars 225–237. The increasing rate of change in a passage of chords I, VI, IV and V leads to eight bars of tonic harmony, brings the overture to a triumphant and noisy end.

Warning. Photocopying any part of this book without permission is illegal.

Private study

1. List the main ingredients that make a 'Rossini crescendo'.
2. What is the difference between sonata form and abridged sonata form?
3. What are the features of a 'stretto'?
4. Suggest a possible reason why the first subject of this comic opera overture is in the minor key.
5. Briefly describe the structure of the slow introduction.
6. What is meant by an antiphonal exchange? Where does one occur in this overture?

Composing

Rossini was a master of witty, entertaining music. Note the elements he uses in the second subject – the simple harmony, clear textures and frequent repetition. Can you make use of these elements in your own composing? They are likely to work more successfully if you are bold and write a piece that is fast-moving in tempo.

Further reading

Rossini by Richard Osborne. *Dent*, 1993. ISBN: 0-460-86103-4.

For an excellent guide to the orchestra in general see **Anatomy of the Orchestra** by Norman Del Mar. *Faber and Faber* 1981, *University of California Press* 1984. ISBN: 0-520-05062-2.

Selected discography

Academy of St Martin in the Fields conducted by Neville Marriner. *EMI CDC7491552*. This includes nine Rossini overtures. Also look out for recordings by Menuhin, Chailly and Abbado.

Orpheus Chamber Orchestra. *Deutsche Grammophon 445569-2*. Exceptionally fine recordings from an orchestra that plays without a conductor. The CD includes eight overtures (and a clarinet work).

Hanover Band conducted by Roy Goodman. *RCA Victor Red Seal 68139-2*. Performances on period instruments of six overtures.

Question practice

1. Compare Rossini's use of the crescendo with Beethoven's use of the same device.
2. Rossini is often accused of being repetitive. To what extent does he vary his material when he repeats it?
3. Compare Rossini's use of wind instruments with Haydn's use of these instruments.
4. Describe some of the different types of orchestral texture available to composers such as Haydn and Rossini.
5. In what ways does this overture establish a comic mood for the opera that is to follow?

A Midsummer Night's Dream — Mendelssohn

Prescribed for examination in 2002–2004

Mendelssohn, born in 1809, was only 17 when he wrote this work in August 1826. Overtures from operas had for many years been played as independent concert pieces, but it was Mendelssohn's innovation to write overtures that were conceived as concert works from the start. *A Midsummer Night's Dream* was the first of a series of such overtures in which he combined illustrative music with sonata form, a structure that was already familiar in instrumental music such as the symphony and the opera overture (see page 46).

Since Mendelssohn provided his publisher with an outline of the features of Shakespeare's play that he reflected in the piece, and because he reworked themes from the overture in the incidental music he wrote for a production of the play in 1843, we can relate almost every element in the overture to Shakespeare's play. However, Mendelssohn himself cautioned that, while the music is indeed closely related to the play, 'the train of thought is, in fact, my overture … if the overture is well written, it can competently speak for itself'.

Instrumentation

The work is written for the standard double-wind orchestra of the time. There are no trombones, but there is one additional and rather unusual instrument, the **ophicleide**, used to strengthen the bass line. This was a bass brass instrument, invented in 1817, that had holes and keys like a woodwind instrument. It was common in military bands and orchestras in the early 19th century and was later superseded by the bass tuba, which has a more rounded sound. The part is played on the tuba on most modern recordings.

The clarinets are in A, so sound a minor 3rd below their written pitches. Thus in bars 86–89 the clarinets are playing exactly the same notes as the flutes and oboes. Trumpets in E sound a major 3rd higher than written as do the horns in E when written in the bass clef, but when in the treble clef the horns transpose in the other direction and sound a minor 6th lower than printed. The horn part in bar 3, for example, sounds E a perfect 5th above the bassoons, while in bar 4 the horns sound E right at the bottom of the texture.

Timpani are tuned to tonic and dominant (E and B) but German scores will give the dominant as H since this is the name given to the note B♮ in German. In the string parts it is worth noticing that while the double basses often play the same notes as the cellos (but sounding an octave lower, of course) they have rather more independence than in the earlier music we have looked at previously.

Shakespeare's play

If possible, try to see Shakespeare's comedy live or on video, or at least read a summary, such as the synopsis in the *Oxford Companion to English Literature*. The plot hinges on the interaction of several different levels of existence. On the one hand there are the mortal worlds of two highly contrasted groups – the aristocrats (notably Theseus, the Duke of Athens, and two pairs of lovers) and some common tradesmen who are called upon to entertain them (notably Bottom, a weaver who is enticed into wearing an ass's head). On the other hand there is the magic world of elves and fairies (notably Oberon and Titania, the King and Queen of the Fairies).

Form	Main keys	Bars
Introduction	e minor	1–5
Exposition	e/E and B	6–250
Development	various	250–394
Recapitulation	e/E	394–620
Coda	e/E	620–686

Listening guide

As we examine the work in detail we will follow its sonata-form outline, but in parallel we will see how Mendelssohn uses various musical ideas within this structure to illustrate aspects of the play.

The first five bars form a brief but magical introduction that later returns like a spell (and certainly not like a normal introduction) at the start of the recapitulation and at the end of the whole piece. Similar sustained wind chords are scattered throughout the overture. These bars open magically from the initial two-part flute chord, through four then six parts to a ten-part tonic chord of E major for wind, but the tonality is shrouded in woodland mist by the use of the minor version of chord IV in the plagal cadence at bars 3–4, and by the change from the tonic major to the tonic minor in bars 4–7. There is no melody to speak of and, with the four successive pauses, no obvious pulse. This is pure sonority. We are here in a timeless zone between reality and magic. In short, this is romantic music.

Exposition Bars 6–250

Having reached E minor we have passed through the open casement into fairyland. The first subject (bars 8–61) is characterised by quiet, fast and insistent quavers played by high and divided (*divisi*) strings in a minor key. Similar devices were so often used by Mendelssohn in his later works that such textures are often colloquially described as his 'fairy music' style. Twice this quicksilver texture is interrupted by a sustained wind chord. Because of the way it is scored it immediately reminds us of the four 'magic' chords at the start. It is as though the fairies have momentarily vanished as quickly as they first appeared.

At bar 62 Mendelssohn introduces another first-subject theme, but now in the tonic major. The contrast of major and minor is vital to his plan, for this represents the contrast in the play – we enter the regal splendour of the court of Theseus, represented by a scalic theme in octaves accompanied by the massive homophonic texture of an orchestral *tutti*. At bar 78 the imitative wind scales heard over a tonic pedal are based on the descending motif of the court theme (see *left*). While the brass sustain the pedal the strings play it in a 'tum-titty-tum' rhythm (bars 78–83). This develops into a short motif in bar 84 and a fully-fledged theme at bar 90. Mendelssohn now turns his texture upside down. Instead of a tonic pedal in the bass he has an inverted dominant pedal played by woodwind and the descending scale appears in the bass. As this transition passage modulates towards the dominant Mendelssohn transforms the fairy music into the major-key world of the mortals (bar 98 onwards), reminding us of how the fairies intervene with the humans in Shakespeare's comedy.

The swooning lyrical melody of bars 130–174 is the second subject, in the dominant key of B major, and represents the lovers. It consists of two four-bar phrases, both of them repeated as though to suggest the complete agreement of the star-crossed Hermia and Lysander. The texture is gradually enriched and repetitions of the second phrase (bars 154–166) become more impassioned with the addition of pedal notes played on horns, the re-entry of clarinets and bassoons and the addition of the ophicleide. After a woodwind and

Warning. Photocopying any part of this book without permission is illegal.

brass fanfare in bars 166–8 the lovers' melody ends with a six-bar phrase played by four-part strings with pizzicato (plucked) double basses supporting a decorated version of a IV–V–I cadence (bars 168–74).

Another second subject theme in B major occupies bars 194–204. This highly contrasting music represents the *bergomask* (country dance) performed by Bottom, Flute, Quince and friends to entertain the aristocrats at court. When Mendelssohn reused this material in his incidental music of 1843 he referred to it much more earthily as a *Rüpeltanz* (a louts' dance!). It is characterised by a crude stomping **double pedal**, in which timpani and ophicleide play a conspicuous role, and by simple-minded repetitions of a three-note motif in the violins. Bottom is given a donkey's head by the fairies and the huge leaps of a 9th and a 10th in the melody sound just like the braying of an ass.

A pedal that consists of two simultaneous pitches, usually tonic and dominant as it is here, is known as a **double pedal**.

The exposition concludes with a codetta (bar 222) that opens with brass fanfares. Notice that tranposition means that the horns sound an octave below the trumpets (see *right*). They represent the Duke's hunting party and their music, taken from bar 70, heralds a reprise of his majestic theme from bar 62, now transposed to B major and starting at bar 230.

After such a wealth of ideas in the exposition, Mendelssohn is now much more economical and concentrates mainly on developing the fairies' music of the first subject. The orchestral textures are often sparse and hushed, and are highly evocative of a midsummer night in an enchanted wood. As the first subject is reduced to nothing more than a cello rhythm (bar 264), sustained woodwind notes remind us of the opening magic chords. The hollow spacing of the diminished 7th chord, with the flutes three octaves above low bassoons, and quivering cellos in the middle, creates the type of ghostly effect beloved of early romantic composers.

Development
Bars 250–394

The first subject reappears in F♯ minor at bar 270, with an accompaniment of delicate detached arpeggios in the woodwind. The sustained chord takes on constantly changing guises like a woodland spirit. It is reduced to a single note for solo cello and bass in bars 276–277 and then it expands through a minor 3rd in very low flutes (bar 283) and a hushed minor-9th chord for strings at bar 284. Above this the motif from bar 90 creeps back like the distant horns of Elfland. Suddenly, at bar 294, the real orchestral horns (instructed to play *con tutta la forza* – with all force) break the dream. Their warning trump sounds twice more as the tonality becomes more fluid, eventually reaching the relatively remote key of D major at bar 316.

Further transformations of the first subject lead to a new texture at bar 334 in which the fairies' quavers are reduced to a reiterated C♯ below which pizzicato strings offer a distant reminder of the descending scales of the court theme. Notice the transparent scoring of bars 342–349 that allows the long *pianissimo* note on unison flutes to be heard, even though it is almost at the bottom of the flute's quietest register. An inversion of the lovers' melody starts in the woodwind at bar 362 and then the development slows and comes to a rest on a chord of C♯ minor in bar 374.

Warning. Photocopying any part of this book without permission is illegal.

Symphonie fantastique (fourth movement)   Berlioz

The shadow of Beethoven hung over early-romantic composers, challenging them to follow his example (if they dared) or to react against it and develop entirely new forms and genres. Berlioz, who was only 25 when Beethoven died, was among the first to take the challenge head on. His *Symphonie fantastique*, first performed in 1830 (just three years after the death of his idol), is cast in five movements, each with a descriptive title, like Beethoven's sixth symphony (the *Pastoral*). He goes further, utilising Beethovenian sonata form, though not the closely argued processes of development apparent in all of Beethoven's symphonies. The revolutionary new elements that caused such a stir in 1830 and which are immediately apparent are:

- explicit, detailed and semi-autobiographical programme notes for every movement, making the work the first true and most influential **programme** symphony of the 19th century
- an orchestral virtuosity that far outstrips the most complex orchestration of earlier composers
- an attempt to unify the whole work by a melody (which Berlioz called an *idée fixe*) that recurs in whole or in part in every movement.

The subtitle of the symphony is 'An episode in the life of an artist'. The artist is Berlioz himself and the episode to which he refers began with a performance of Shakespeare's *Hamlet* in which a beautiful actress named Harriet Smithson played Ophelia. Berlioz fell passionately in love with her, and he describes in his diaries how obsessive his fixation became, almost driving him to the point of suicide. The *idée fixe* (literally a 'fixed idea', but used in French to mean an obsession) represents Harriet. Berlioz wrote a detailed programme note that he asked be distributed to every member of the audience and said it 'should be treated as the spoken text of an opera, serving as introductions to the musical movements and explaining their character and expression'. For the fourth movement, *Marche au supplice* (March to the guillotine) it reads:

> Knowing beyond doubt that his love is unrequited the artist poisons himself with opium. The dose of the drug, too weak to kill him, plunges him into a sleep disturbed by the most horrible visions. He dreams he has killed the one he loves, that he has been condemned to death, taken to the place of punishment, and that he witnesses his own execution. The cortege processes to the sounds of a march, now sombre and fierce, now brilliant and solemn, in which the dull thud of heavy footsteps are suddenly followed by the most startling outbursts of sound. At the end of the march the first four bars of the *idée fixe* reappear like a last thought of love interrupted by the fatal blow.

The 'dull thud of heavy footsteps' in slow march time is portrayed by divided double basses and a lugubrious horn motif at the start of the movement. The march tune starting in bar 17 is truly 'fierce' (at the start) and 'sombre' (at the end) and is interrupted by 'a most startling outburst' at bar 40, and a second march tune (bar 62) is indeed 'brilliant'. These themes alternate in increasingly frantic orchestral textures until the condemned man reaches 'Madame Guillotine' and, in an expectant silence, remembers his lost love

---

Programme music is, in its most typical form, music which attempts to tell a story. The story tends to dictate the form and so programme music is rather different to the illustrative style of music that we saw Mendelssohn used in his overture, *A Midsummer Night's Dream*.

(bars 164–8). In bar 169 we hear 'chop, drop, bounce, bounce' as the hero is decapitated and his head falls and bounces into the basket. Finally the jubilation of the vindictive spectators (among them the horrified composer who has just witnessed his own execution in his nightmare) is represented by tremendous rolls on three timpani and side drum, together with brilliantly scored chords of G major.

This realistic blow-by-blow account of events is the origin of many such passages in later programme music and its highly personalised style of expression is just one of many features that should help you recognise that Berlioz is a romantic composer, far removed in outlook from the elegant style of the composers of the late 18th century.

Berlioz was a master of instrumentation and he wrote the first important book on the subject (*Grand traité d'instrumentation*). The orchestra for the *Symphonie fantastique* is considerably larger than any requires in the earlier works we have studied. The woodwind section requires four bassoons, not two, and in various parts of the work he uses piccolo, cor anglais and the little E♭ clarinet.

Brass (and percussion) play a much more prominent role in this work than in earlier symphonies. There are four valve horns and, in addition to the usual two trumpets, Berlioz specifies two *cornets à pistons* – valved brass instruments which have a full chromatic range. This explains why, in passages such as bars 94–6, the cornets play the melody while the trumpeters have to be content with accompanimental parts. In addition to three trombones Berlioz requires two bass brass instruments. Originally these were the raucous sounds of the ophicleide (see page 55) and the serpent – an instrument with a snake-like tube and finger-holes – but Berlioz later sanctioned the use of the smoother-toned tuba.

The percussion section requires two timpanists to play four kettle-drums (they are used in four-part chords near the end of the third movement). *Piatti* are cymbals and *gran cassa* is a bass drum. The 'tamb.' which enters in bar 170 is a *tamburo militare* (military drum – the modern side drum or snare drum) not a tambourine. Finally, to balance all of this, Berlioz specifies in great detail at the start of the first movement that he requires at least 60 string players – making a total minimum force of some 90 players.

Berlioz included many detailed performance directions in his score. These are reproduced in full in editions such as the Norton Critical Score but in other editions some may be abbreviated or omitted. For example, at the start not only are the timpani instructed to play with *baguettes d'éponge* (sponge-headed drum sticks) but Berlioz added 'The first quaver of each [minim] beat should be played with both drum sticks, the other five with the right-hand drum stick.' The horns in bar two are instructed to 'play the stopped notes with the hand without using the valves'. Stopped notes are produced by adjusting the position of the hand in the bell so that the pitch is lowered by up to a semitone. The technique causes the tone colour to become muted and thin, and Berlioz exploits this as an expressive device perhaps to suggest the half-light of a grey dawn through which the cortege makes its way to the place of execution.

Instrumentation

The first and second horns are in B♭ basso (German scores describe B♭ as B). These sound a major 9th lower than printed. The horns in E♭ (Es in German terminology) sound a major 6th lower than printed. This will become clearer if you compare the first example printed on the next page with the same bars in your own score.

Form	Main keys	*Bars*
Introduction	g minor	1–16
Exposition	g/B♭	17–77
Development and Recapitulation	g/B♭	78–164
Coda	g/G	164–178

Listening guide

On Score.

The 'March to the Scaffold' contains a fairly regular sonata-form exposition but Berlioz rolls the development and recapitulation into one lengthy section that balances the repeated exposition. From a tonal point of view the movement is remarkably unadventurous. Most of it is in G minor or its relative major (B♭) and it ends in G major. Apart from a sudden plunge into D♭ major at bar 130 the only other key that Berlioz visits is E♭ major (bars 31–46).

Introduction Bars 1–16

The highly original opening with two very quiet kettledrums a minor third apart creates an indistinct, menacing timbre, while the sponge-headed timpani sticks provide a muffled tone quality in keeping with the funereal nature of the march. Pizzicato double basses, divided into four groups, highlight the pulse with dense *pianissimo* chords. These sound an octave lower than printed so, like the timpani, their pitches are indistinct. The result (motif *x*) is a sound effect that mimics the 'dull thud of heavy footsteps'.

Stopped horns introduce a syncopated pattern (motif *y*) that begins hesitatingly, alternating with motif *x*. This leads to a crescendo over a dominant seventh (bars 13–16) and a perfect cadence is formed by overlapping the end of the introduction with the start of the first subject in bar 17. Notice how the bottom note of the dominant chord is actually the 7th (the lowest double-bass note), here used purely to give weight to the texture – there is no sign of it resolving down a semitone in conventional textbook fashion.

It was for such harmonic 'irregularities' as this that Berlioz was often criticised by the conservative musical establishment of Paris. A reviewer of the first performance wrote 'I saw that his harmony is composed by piling up tones into monstrous heaps ... and I came to the conclusion that he would always write in a barbaric manner'.

Exposition Bars 17–77

The first subject consists of the simple descending scale of G melodic minor announced by cellos and basses in octaves. Berlioz, for all his innovations, has his roots firmly in the classical tradition – notice that it is an eight-bar phrase ending with an imperfect cadence in bar 24. The whole of the first part of the exposition consists of repetitions of this theme set against a variety of counter-melodies. In bars 25–32 the theme (played in parallel 3rds by lower strings) is set against a countermelody on all four bassoons in unison, characterised by dotted rhythms as it modulates to a perfect cadence in E♭ major. In bars 33–40 the theme (played in octaves by violins) is accompanied by a second countermelody played in octaves by lower strings. It ends with an imperfect cadence in E♭ major, above which is heard the first of the 'startling outbursts of sound' played by syncopated wind.

Bars 41–49 are a repeat of bars 33–39 but a rapid modulation and a perfect cadence effects a return to the tonic key of G minor in bar 49. Over the cadence pattern Berlioz supplies another 'startling outburst', and this time the syncopation is intensified by the use of **diminution** (the notes and rests are half the length they were previously). In bars 49–56 the theme (on cellos and double basses) is combined with its inversion (on violins and violas). This **mirror inversion** is accompanied by a third countermelody of continuous quavers played by all four bassoons.

A series of perfect cadences in G minor (bars 55–60) leads abruptly to the second subject in B♭ major (the relative major). Although there is no transition between the first and second subjects they are linked by the octave B♭s played by an ophicleide (or tuba) in

Warning. Photocopying any part of this book without permission is illegal.

bars 60–65. The second subject, announced by the wind with off-beat timpani, is based on motif *y* from the introduction. It consists of two almost identical eight-bar phrases, the first ending with an imperfect cadence (bar 69), the second ending with a perfect cadence (bar 77), thus forming periodic phrasing with balanced antecedent and consequent.

At bar 62 the horns are instructed to play unmuted – a more powerful and brilliant timbre ('The cortege processes to the sound of a march … now brilliant and solemn'). In this section the third trombone is assigned a low B♭. This is known as a pedal note – a very low note, below the range normally used, which has a crude, rasping effect. It should not be confused with the harmonic device known as a pedal, although here the B♭ does also function as a tonic pedal. The whole introduction and exposition is (or should be) repeated.

In his treatise on orchestration Berlioz wrote 'I have used the pedal notes of the tenor trombone [because] I wanted the lower harmonies to sound extremely harsh'. He was one of the first composers to exploit effects of this sort.

Berlioz sets up an antiphonal exchange between brass and woodwind using rhythms from the first subject. These homophonic textures are enlivened by the strings. Their rhythm derives from motif *x*, but here the accents at the start of each sextuplet are reinforced by dissonant appoggiaturas (G resolving to F♯ and E♭ resolving to D).

Development and Recapitulation
Bars 78–164

At bar 82 the first subject is recapitulated in the tonic key, but its descending scale is now presented with constant changes of tone colour and octave in a way that seems to anticipate 20th-century techniques of instrumentation:

Berlioz thus creates a grotesque parody of a theme which, in its original form he described as 'fierce and sombre'. The music modulates to B♭ major for a rescored repeat of the whole of the second subject in its original key (bars 89–104). Although the theme in the wind parts remains virtually unchanged, Berlioz adds string parts that again anticipate a technique most often associated with 20th-century composers. It consists of the simultaneous combination of two or more conflicting rhythmic patterns, a technique known as **polyrhythm**. The continuous semiquavers in the violins cut across the triplets of the violas and cellos. These in turn conflict with the dotted rhythms of the double basses. To the ear the effect is an almost palpable evocation of a madly whirling crowd in a drug-induced vision of hell – which is, of course, precisely the effect Berlioz intended to create.

Bars 105–113 are a repeat of bars 78–85 with some changes to the orchestration, followed by a one-bar link. Sequential development of the descending scale from the first subject occurs in low brass and woodwind at bar 114. Against this the double basses steadily rise from G to F♯ (the leading note), finally reaching their goal (the upper tonic) in bar 123. The other strings decorate this scale with slides (notated as small grace notes) while upper wind decorate the same idea with sextuplets (derived from motif *x*). This simultaneous combination of a simple melody with ornamented versions of itself is known as **heterophony** and is used as an expressive device that helps build towards the climax in bar 123. As this approaches timpani are instructed to play with *baguettes de bois* (wooden drum sticks) to produce a harder sound and flutes ascend chromatically while basses descend diatonically. This all leads to the return of the first subject in bar 123. The expected perfect cadence at the end of this reprise is interrupted by another 'startling outburst', with trumpets and drums on F and everyone else on C♯. The latter note, renamed as D♭, is used as a pivot note to introduce the totally unrelated key of D♭ major. Bar 131 sees an inversion of the first subject in this key followed by a modulation leading to a perfect cadence in the tonic key of G minor (bar 140).

Berlioz then develops the dotted-note figures from the second subject (first heard at bars 63–64) in G minor. The violins are instructed to play this passage on their lowest string. Wind highlight the rhythm with a tonic pedal and snappy perfect cadences. A chromatic then diatonic descent in bars 152–3 is interrupted by the dotted figure, now reduced to repeated chords in the same rhythm. The interpolation of the unrelated chord of D♭ major (bar 155) between a G-minor scale and a G-minor chord was so unusual that Berlioz was obliged to add a footnote clarifying 'there is no misprint here'. The section ends with two definitive perfect cadences in the tonic key of G minor (bars 160–161 and 163–164). Notice that in bar 157 the first timpanist is instructed to change the pitch of the larger of his two drums from B♭ to B♮ ready for the end of the movement.

Coda
Bars 164–178

The *idée fixe* appears for the first and only time in this movement, presented as a **monophonic** texture (that is, a single melodic line without accompaniment) by a solo clarinet. Berlioz highlights the anguish of the moment with the Italian phrase *dolce assai e appassionato* (very sweet and impassioned). This is immediately followed by the decapitation in G minor (bar 169). Although not printed in all editions, Berlioz wrote on the cymbal part *étouffez le son* (stop the sound), which is done by pressing the vibrating cymbals against the body, and on the bass drum part, *étouffez le son avec la main* (stop the sound with the hand), both directions ensuring that the *fortissimo* crash is curtailed quickly enough to allow the pizzicato strings to be heard. Finally an awe-inspiring roll performed by snare drums (Berlioz wanted two of them) and three timpani playing a G-major chord supports a colossal orchestral build-up in which the wind, and then everyone else, piles on successive G-major chords to create a sheer wall of sound.

Private study

1. Why is this work regarded as revolutionary?
2. What is an *idée fixe* and how is it used by Berlioz?
3. What instruments does Berlioz use that were not normally used in the symphony orchestra of the time?
4. Which unusual instrument does Berlioz use that was also used by Mendelssohn in the overture you have studied?
5. What is unusual about the way Berlioz uses sonata form in this movement?

Groupwork

Each student should research, and prepare short notes on, the development of one particular instrument in the period 1780–1830. As far as possible it is best if everyone chooses an instrument that they themselves play. Try to establish *why* developments took place and the effect they had on the music being composed during this period. Present your findings to the rest of the group.

In group discussion consider the question 'Can music tell a story?', referring to various pieces of illustrative and programme music that you know.

Composing

Telling a story in music is relatively easy, but form needs careful consideration if you are not to end up with a series of sound effects that are totally perplexing to the listener. If you are tempted to try a piece of programme music keep the content very simple and remember that it is the music that must be the prime focus.

Further reading

Berlioz: Orchestral Music by Hugh McDonald. *BBC Consumer Publishing (Books)*, 1969. ISBN: 0-563-08455-3. This handy BBC Music Guide sometimes goes out of print, but it can often be found in libraries and second-hand bookshops.

Berlioz, Fantastic Symphony edited by Edward T. Cone. *W. W. Norton*, 1971. ISBN: 0-393-09926-1. This Norton Critical Score of the work includes historical background.

Berlioz by Hugh McDonald. *Oxford University Press*, 1994. ISBN: 0-460-86052-6. See chapter 9 and the last six pages of chapter 5.

Discography

Concertgebouw Orchestra conducted by Colin Davis. *Philips 446 202-2*. This famous recording from 1974 is now available as a mid-price CD. Also look out for recordings by Stokowski, Bernstein, Klemperer and Muti.

Orchestre révolutionnaire et romantique conducted by John Eliot Gardiner. *Philips 434 402-2*. Try to hear this spectacular recording on period instruments made in the hall in which the symhony was first heard. You will have no difficulty in spotting the ophicleide!

Question practice

1. Berlioz's *Symphonie fantastique* was written four years after Mendelssohn's overture *A Midsummer Night's Dream*. How does Berlioz's use of innovative orchestral techniques differ from Mendelssohn's?

2. How does Berlioz's orchestration capture the mood of a 'march to the scaffold'?

3. Outline the growth of the orchestra from the time of Mozart to the time of Berlioz.

4. How does the type of programme music used by Berlioz differ from the illustrative style of music that Mendelssohn used in his overture *A Midsummer Night's Dream*?

5. Discuss some of the more unusual playing techniques and orchestral effects used by Berlioz, and state how effective you think these are in the context of this work.

Jazz

Jazz has developed at an astonishing rate in its short history, and the speed of this development has left us a wide range of recorded music to study. The period on which we focus, 1920 to 1960, saw rapid change in the music and also in the experience of African-Americans in the United States. Jazz began in the southern city of New Orleans and its earliest recordings are in **New Orleans style**. The music then travelled up through Chicago to New York as black Americans sought better economic and social conditions in the more liberal northern cities. This was accompanied by rapid technological advances which contributed to the wide dissemination of music by gramophone record and radio broadcasts. The vitality of the music reflected the new opportunities in American society, and the 1920s became known as 'the Jazz Age'.

Throughout the 1930s and 1940s jazz was the dominant popular dance style, and **big bands** that played **swing** were extremely well supported. However, in this extremely commercial field, some of the more interesting musicians such as Duke Ellington were passed over in favour of bandleaders who were orientated towards show business, and big-band music began to suffer from rigidity and cliché. Jazz musicians in New York reacted to this by formulating a complex new style that became known as **bebop**.

Bebop was important in establishing jazz as music for listening rather than for dancing – an important change that led to the emergence of **cool jazz** in the early fifties. At this point rock and roll started to become the main type of dance music and this gave jazz players the freedom to extend their musical ideas in jazz clubs or concert halls. At the same time the advent of the long-playing record, offering 20 minutes per side, allowed jazz musicians to record extensive improvisations and for the first time to capture the music as it was played in live performance.

The conventions of jazz performance

Before looking at the specified works in detail, it is important to understand some of the conventions that have developed in jazz performing, arranging and composing, and the language used by jazz musicians to describe them.

Instrumentation

The line-up of a jazz ensemble is divided into two groups:

+ The **frontline**. These are the instruments that take a melodic role, usually wind instruments such as saxophones, trumpets or trombones, but there can also be other instruments such as violin or vibraphone. In big bands, such as the Duke Ellington Orchestra, these frontline instruments are organised in trumpet, trombone and **reed** sections.

+ The **rhythm section**. These are the instruments that provide a rhythmic and harmonic accompaniment for the frontline. The instrumentation differs from era to era but there is almost always a chordal instrument (such as piano, guitar or banjo) a bass instrument (such as tuba or double bass) and a drum kit (usually

> In jazz the term **reeds** refers primarily to saxophones and clarinets, but is also used to include the flute since, if it is required, it is usually played by a saxophonist.

> Warning. Photocopying any part of this book without permission is illegal.

consisting of pedal bass drum, snare drum, tom-toms, hi-hat and cymbals). At the time of some earlier recordings, such as Louis Armstrong's *West End Blues*, the drum kit was still evolving, and doesn't include all of the above.

The rhythm section players each have a specific role, outlined below, and they generally play all the time whereas the frontline players dip in and out of the music.

- **Comping** is the rhythmic playing of chords on piano, guitar or banjo in support of a theme or a solo. The rhythms and voicings of the chords are usually improvised, and in some bands more than one instrument may take this role.

- **Walking** is a style of bass playing developed in the early 1930s in which the bass player plays an on-the-beat crotchet line. This outlines the harmony by using notes of the chord, often filled in with passing notes. The example *right* shows a walking bass formed from a G^7 chord with * indicating the passing notes.

- **Time** is played by the drummer, whose job is to generate the pulse of the music, often by playing loosely repeated patterns on ride cymbal and hi-hat. The drummer also colours the music by use of the many sounds available from a drum kit, and also interacts with soloist and other rhythm section players, usually by playing snare drum phrases.

Having seen how the instruments are divided, we should examine what materials the players have to work with, and how they manipulate them.

Form

The most common structure used in jazz is **variation** form. There is generally a harmonised theme or melody known as the **head**. The pattern of chords, called the **changes**, that accompanies the theme is then repeated by the rhythm section while a series of soloists improvise new melodic lines to fit the harmonies. Each repeat of the pattern is known as a **chorus**. The theme is then repeated, and this is known as the 'out chorus'. There may be a short introduction at the beginning of the piece, and there may also be a coda at the end. So the format for many jazz performances is that which is summarised in the box, *right*.

> Intro
>
> **Head** (establishes chord pattern)
>
> **Solos** (based on chord pattern)
>
> **Head** (or 'out chorus')
>
> **Coda**

Until the 1960s jazz musicians mainly used the **12-bar blues** and the **24- or 32-bar popular song** (songs known as standards) as a basis for the changes. We can see the former in *Ko-ko* (set for study in 2001–2) or *Straight No Chaser* (set for 2003–4) and the latter in *Rockin' in Rhythm* and *Move* (both set for 2003–4).

Rhythm

Rhythm is the most important element in jazz, and the one which really defines the music in relation to other popular musical forms. Jazz began as dance music and remained such until the early 1950s. During this time nearly all jazz had either two or four beats to the bar and changes in meter were extremely rare. However within this seemingly rigid framework one can find infinite variation. The combined rhythmic language of west-African and European dance traditions gave jazz a rhythmic buoyancy and propulsion which became known as **swing**. This is characterised by subdividing the beat not into two even quavers, as is so common in classical music,

Written

Played

Written

Played

Basic pulse

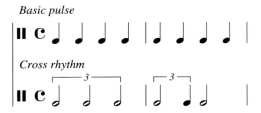

Cross rhythm

but into long–short groupings known as **swing quavers**. These are fiddly to express in notation, so they are usually written as even quavers even though in performance they are played in more of an uneven triplet pattern, as shown in the first example *left*. There is often an accent on the last note in the bar, as shown in the second example. The music is propelled by the accented anticipation and delay of the main beats of the bar, a practice known as **syncopation**.

Notation that developed for classical music does not adapt easily to showing the finer nuances of jazz rhythm and it is worth noting that experienced jazz players place great importance on getting to *feel* the rhythmic 'groove' rather than trying to 'read the dots'.

Jazz musicians often increase the intensity of their improvisations by playing swing *semiquavers* over the basic crotchet pulse, a device known as **double time** because it can suggest a doubling of the pulse. Listen to saxophonists Cannonball Adderley and John Coltrane in *All Blues* for an example of this. Another common device is **cross rhythm**. This usually consists of three-against-two rhythms (see *left*). An example of cross-rhythm can be heard in the second chorus of Bill Evans' piano solo on the same track.

Harmony

For most jazz musicians the underlying chord sequence is more important than the melody of the theme. All of the musicians, not just the players of chordal instruments, must know and understand the changes thoroughly in order to improvise upon them. While the length of the pattern and the position of main cadence points invariably remain unchanged, jazz musicians may **substitute** one chord for another, or change basic chord qualities (such as adding a 6th instead of a 7th). The other players, on hearing this, may respond by altering their own contribution, or may incorporate this addition at the same point in the following chorus. Chord patterns are not *completely* fixed events but are fluid and adaptable, according to what is happening in the music at any given point.

A **chord substitution** is the replacement of a chord by one with a similar harmonic function (e.g. as a tonic, dominant or subdominant). For example instead of chord IV a jazz musician might use II^7 or a minor version of chord IV or perhaps a complex chromatic chord that has only a single note in common with chord IV.

Blues harmony in jazz

Blues music pre-dates jazz and has had a strong influence on its development in terms of sound and melodic line, which we will look at below, and through the use of the blues sequence, a chord pattern that has had a profound effect on western popular music in the 20th century. The composers of four of the six jazz pieces in this book have used the structure of the 12-bar blues sequence:

bars	1	2	3	4	5	6	7	8	9	10	11	12
West End Blues (E♭)	I	I	I	I^7	IV	IV	I	I	V^7	V^7	I	I
Ko-ko (E♭ minor)	I^6	I^6	I^6	I^6	IV^6	IV^6	I^6	I^6	V^7	V^7	I	I
All Blues (G)	I^7	I^7	I^7	I^7	Im^7	Im^7	I^7	I^7	V^7	$♭IV^7$–V^7	I^7	I^7
Straight No Chaser (G)	I^7	I^7	I^7	I^7	IV^7	IV^7	I^7	I^7	IIm^7	I^7	I^7–V^7	IIm^7–V^7

Because it is an oral folk form, the blues sequence has never been fixed, and over the years its fluid nature has allowed composers and improvisers to alter some elements. Notice the various chord qualities depending on style and era:

✦ *West End Blues* has predominantly triadic harmony, with the occasional use of dominant 7ths

- *Ko-ko* has major 6ths added to the minor triads I and IV
- *All Blues* has flattened 7ths added to all chords, giving a restless quality, plus some chromatic notes for colour
- *Straight No Chaser* has more harmonic movement in the last four bars to add momentum to the end of each chorus.

However certain patterns are constant in all four recordings:

- the chord sequence begins with four bars of chord I
- there is a movement to chord IV in the fifth bar of the sequence (implied in *All Blues* by the change from I major to I minor)
- there is a return to chord I in the seventh bar
- there is a move to chord V in the ninth bar (in *Straight No Chaser* this is delayed by IIm^7 which then leads to V in bar 10)
- there is a return to chord I in bar eleven.

One curious feature of blues harmony to bear in mind is the fact that chord I is treated like a *dominant* chord; if a 7th is added it will be the *flattened* 7th, which can have the effect of making chord IV temporarily sound like the tonic of the subdominant key. Another important aspect is the way that improvisers often ignore blues harmony, using one set of pitches over all of the chords. This can be heard in the first chorus trombone theme of *Ko-ko*.

C major: I$^{♭7}$ IV
F major: V^7 I

Improvisation

Often jazz musicians will play without any notated music at all. Rhythm section players improvise their accompaniment, carrying the harmonic sequence in their heads and interacting with the other musicians in a conversational way. Similarly, in the statement of the theme the frontline players may personalise the melody by decorating it or altering its phrasing and rhythm (for instance, Louis Armstrong's rendition of the first full chorus of *West End Blues*). This is known as **paraphrase improvisation** and is more common in smaller groups than in the bigger bands where the themes tend to be more tightly organised.

After the first statement of the theme the soloist will often spontaneously construct an alternative melodic line, accompanied by the rhythm section.

The ways in which the soloist can approach improvising include:

- using part of the original theme as a basis for variations, for example Louis Armstrong in *West End Blues*
- establishing a new melodic or rhythmic idea and then developing this motif, for example Miles Davis in *All Blues*
- using the underlying harmony as the main organising principle, for example Johnny Coles in *Straight No Chaser*.

Other considerations for the improviser may include:

- creating moments of calm and periods of activity
- contrasting scale-based and interval-based ideas
- balancing consonant and dissonant elements
- phrasing within or across formal units such as four-bar sections
- using techniques such as double time or cross rhythm.

Improvisers rarely use one approach exclusively and are much more likely to combine different ideas. All of the great soloists in jazz have developed an individual approach to improvising which distinguishes them from other players and which can be identified by features such as harmonic language and phrasing, as well as the character of their instrumental sound.

Sound and instrumental technique

Jazz demands virtuosic musicianship of its players, and they in turn value individuality and innovation very highly. Consequently they have been keenly involved in the transformation of instrumental sounds and in extending the technique of their instruments. A major factor in the distinctive sound of good jazz musicians is their awareness of fine gradations in pitch. This is a direct result of the influence of the subtle inflections of pitch found in the blues.

Blues is a vocal style in which singers routinely 'bend' the pitch of certain notes for expressive effect. This often happens when approaching the major 3rd of the key, when the singer will hit the minor 3rd and then slide up to the major 3rd. Similarly the 5th and the 7th of the scale may be approached from the semitone below. The term **blue note** is used by jazz musicians to describe a minor 3rd against a major chord, but it can also apply to the technique of playing a note pitched *between* the major and minor 3rd. These vocally-based inflections are widespread in jazz, and occur in all of the prescribed works, particularly in trombone solos where the use of the slide enables microtonal shifts in imitation of a voice.

Wind players in jazz also imitate the human voice in their use of vibrato and wide range of articulation and attack. An extensive range of mutes is used by brass players to colour the sound and the rhythm section is similarly creative in coming up with new ways to play instruments. Jazz players were responsible for originating a cohesive approach to drum-kit technique, developing the extensive use of pizzicato in double-bass playing and establishing the electric guitar as a lead instrument.

Jazz composing and arranging

It is important to understand the difference between arranging and composing in jazz. Many works for smaller groups simply consist of a melodic line and chord pattern which is then spontaneously fleshed out in performance by the players, as in *West End Blues*. Some jazz composers write themes primarily as vehicles for improvising, as a kind of launch pad for the soloists. The original version of *Straight No Chaser*, recorded by pianist Thelonious Monk in 1951, was a one-chorus blues head, but arranger Gil Evans has taken this theme and extended it so that it unfolds over five choruses.

Many jazz compositions are based on existing chord sequences. *Move*, for instance, is based on a hybrid of Gershwin's *I Got Rhythm* and Fats Waller's *Honeysuckle Rose*. The musicians have at their disposal a pool of widely known harmonic sequences based on such songs. Over these they devise fresh themes and thus create new contexts for their improvising. Often the original melody does not appear at all, partly to help avoid performing-rights problems in using copyright songs. Duke Ellington developed a more integrated and organic approach to jazz composition, in which he incorporated the improvisations of his band members into the texture of the music. However in general it can be seen that jazz is essentially a cooperative creative activity in which it is rarely appropriate to think in terms of a single composer.

When listening to recordings, especially older ones where sound quality may not be too good, the music can seem remote. However remember that in its day this was cutting edge music that was made predominantly by young people. The foundations of black American popular music were laid by these musicians, and many of their innovations have passed into common use in all sorts of other music. Having originated in America, jazz is now a global music, with leading players from Britain, Scandinavia, South Africa and many other countries. In Britain there are radio programs dedicated to various jazz styles, and in some areas there are jazz radio stations. Similarly most large record stores will have a jazz department.

But in order to really understand the spontaneity of jazz, it is essential to see a band playing live rather than just listening to CDs. Most larger towns have a pub or arts centre where bands play, or failing that there are many commercially-available videos of well known jazz artists. We can analyse what an improviser played on a recording and assume certain things, but seeing the process happening in the moment is the only way to understand the relationship between the musicians, and to grasp that each performance is unique in its balance of beauty and imperfection.

Jazz today

Jazz FM broadcasts in London, some other parts of the country and via the internet. Programme schedules can be found on their website at http://www.jazzfm.co.uk/

BBC Radio 3 regularly broadcasts jazz, see http://www.bbc.co.uk/radio3/jazz/ for more details and listings.

http://www.notz.com/ukjazz.htm is just one of many websites carrying news about jazz in the UK, including jazz festivals and links to other sites containing jazz information.

For national listings of jazz gigs, news and information about jazz in education see the website http://www.jazzservices.org.uk/

A note on transcriptions. The majority of the music discussed here was created without the use of notation. The transcriptions in this guide are an attempt to aid listening and understanding by representing some sounds on the page. Because of the subtleties of tonal inflection, rhythmic placement and phrasing in these performances, the transcriptions are by definition a *reduction* of the music and the recordings should always be treated as the primary 'text'.

Private study

Answer the following questions which are based on this chapter.

1. What instruments are played by the rhythm section players and what are their main roles?
2. What is the difference between the head and the changes?
3. Explain the meaning of the term 'swing quavers'.
4. What were the two main influences that the blues had on jazz?
5. In what ways have jazz musicians changed the traditional sound of their instruments?

Further reading

Jazz Styles: History and Analysis by Mark C. Gridley. *Prentice Hall*, seventh edition 1999. ISBN: 0-13-021227-X. A comprehensive but concise American textbook with many definitions and clear explanations of how the music works. CD included.

What to Listen for in Jazz by Barry Kernfeld. *Yale University Press*, 1955. ISBN: 0-300-07259-7. A detailed account of the conventions of jazz performance with a CD and transcriptions.

The New Grove Dictionary of Jazz edited by Barry Kernfeld. *Macmillan*, 1994. ISBN: 0-333-63231-1. This single-volume version of the original two-volume edition is good value and includes much about the elements of jazz as well as information on the prescribed works.

Warning. Photocopying any part of this book without permission is illegal.

Prescribed for examination in 2001 and 2002 **West End Blues**   **Louis Armstrong (1928)**

New Orleans and the birth of jazz

At the start of the 20th century, New Orleans was a vibrant, international sea port with a rich mix of nationalities and cultures, resulting in a strong tradition of varied music making. There was a unique blend of marching bands, light-classical and salon music, ragtime, blues, visiting Mexican dance bands, and the combined legacy of west-African and European folk forms. There was a glut of cheap instruments that became available when thousands of Union troops stationed in and around the city during the American civil war were disbanded. And importantly, there was work for black musicians in the busy prostitution district of Storyville, where they played dance music long into the night.

This was the musical environment into which **Louis Armstrong** was born in 1901. Armstrong's early years were extremely deprived, and in his teens he was sent to the Home for Colored Waifs for his delinquent behaviour. Here he began to play cornet, and his innate ability enabled him to progress very quickly and obtain work, first with Kid Ory and then with the Creole Jazz Band. His mentor, Joe 'King' Oliver (composer of *West End Blues*) played first cornet in this band and Armstrong played second cornet.

The Creole Jazz Band played in typical early New Orleans style in which the lead instruments wove a semi-improvised texture of melodic lines around a loose and often unnotated theme. The frontline players took very specific roles in these ensembles:

- the trumpet or cornet took the theme
- the clarinet provided a continuous decorative line above the trumpet
- the trombone played a slower-moving tenor countermelody and sometimes doubled the bass line.

The term **break** simply means a short and unaccompanied solo.

Improvisations were often collective, with individual contributions submerged in the general texture of the music, except for the occasional two-bar **break** at the end of a section. At these points, all players but one would abruptly stop on a short, accented chord and leave the solo instrument playing in a spirited and lively way. Rhythm sections varied in instrumentation from band to band, but commonly included piano and/or banjo, tuba and a primitive version of what we now call a drum kit.

New Orleans wind players were very keen on altering the basic instrumental timbre and liked to use microtonal inflections to imitate the human voice in various ways. They would:

Try not to confuse glissando, which refers to a rapid series of adjacent notes, with a slide (*portamento*) in which the pitch glides between notes. You can perform a glissando on the piano but you cannot play *portamento*.

- glissando up to notes or fall in pitch at the end of the note
- slide between two pitches (*portamento*)
- decorate long notes with turns and trills
- use vibrato that could vary in speed and intensity from note to note
- vary the volume and attack from note to note to create speech-like phrasing.

Warning. Photocopying any part of this book without permission is illegal.

Chicago in the 1920s

In 1918 the slums and brothels of Storyville were bulldozed by the authorities, and New Orleans musicians had to look elsewhere for employment. Many moved to Chicago, including Armstrong and Oliver, and here their music was recorded for the first time. Through these recordings, Louis Armstrong became known as a prodigiously gifted improviser, and he went on to make 60 or so recordings as a band leader between 1925 and 1928. Known as the Hot Fives and Hot Sevens after the names of his bands, these records had a profound effect on the development of jazz.

The 1928 recording of *West End Blues* represents the consolidation of his late New Orleans style and is representative of a shift away from the practice of collective improvisation in earlier recordings. As Armstrong's considerable abilities developed, his dramatic improvisations, and to some extent those of his colleagues, were increasingly a focal point. They were given space to shine in a more transparent texture of rhythm-section accompaniment and sustained notes from the other frontline players, if they played at all. This pushed the soloist to the fore, and as a consequence jazz improvisation developed beyond the practice of paraphrasing or decorating a theme. Led by Armstrong's example, soloists began to improvise away from the thematic material, establishing new melodic ideas in their improvisations, using the harmonies as a basis for melodic ideas, and implying alternative harmonies. This became the established convention in small group instrumental jazz that was to remain unaltered for another 30 years or so.

Private study

1. What were the conditions in New Orleans that enabled jazz to develop?
2. What was the instrumentation of New Orleans-style jazz and what were the frontline roles?
3. How did Armstrong's playing change the format of early jazz?

The arrangement

West End Blues consists of five choruses of a slow blues in E♭ major, with a solo introduction and short coda. The theme is loosely stated in the first and last choruses, but Armstrong's rendition of it is so intertwined with his own improvised gestures that it is impossible to separate the two. There is no formal arrangement in the sense of an individual arranger deciding how instruments should combine and what notes they should play. Instead there is a collective agreement about what goes where, and a spontaneous fleshing out of the basic theme and accompanying harmonies. The use of different instrumental combinations from chorus to chorus produces a great deal of textural variety:

✦ solo trumpet (introduction) and solo piano (fourth chorus)
✦ soloist with rhythm-section accompaniment (second chorus)
✦ two soloists with rhythm-section accompaniment (third chorus)
✦ all three frontline players with rhythm-section accompaniment (fifth chorus).

West End Blues

Composed by Joe 'King' Oliver and Clarence Williams. Recorded 6 June 1928 in Chicago by Louis Armstrong and his Hot Five.

Trumpet and vocal: Louis Armstrong
Clarinet: Jimmy Strong
Trombone: Fred Robinson
Piano: Earl Hines
Banjo: Mancy Cara
Drums: Zutty Singleton

Warning. Photocopying any part of this book without permission is illegal.

Form
Intro
Chorus 1   Theme (trumpet)
Chorus 2   Trombone solo
Chorus 3   Clarinet and vocal duet
Chorus 4   Piano solo
Chorus 5   Theme (trumpet)
Coda

The basic on-the-beat comping is varied in the second chorus by the addition of percussion and rolling tremolo chords on the piano. Further variety is added by Armstrong's wordless improvised singing in the third chorus. The performance is made more interesting by the controlled ebb and flow of the dynamic level, building to a peak in the fifth chorus with the insistent sound of the trumpet in its higher register, and by the way that the steady pulse of the blues choruses contrast with the freely phrased intro and ending.

Listening guide

To help you follow the music the timings of the main events are shown in the form 1:24, meaning one minute 24 seconds from the start. However the form should be clear after listening a few times, so try to rely on your ears rather than your watch or CD counter.

Time 0:00 **Intro** The recording starts with an emphatic, cadenza-like passage for unaccompanied trumpet in which Armstrong confidently uses almost the full range of the instrument:

There are two distinct ideas, an opening arpeggiated fanfare first falling and then rising to an assured top C, in an elegant U-shaped phrase, contrasting with the intricate double time of the gradually descending scalic phrase which follows.

Much has been written about this introduction, one of the most famous moments in the history of recorded jazz. Such a bold and daring style was common in light-classical cornet cadenzas of the time and was characteristic of the brass playing in Mexican bands heard in New Orleans, but it was an innovation in jazz.

Tonality Notice the subtle tonal ambiguity of this unaccompanied opening, which is introducing a blues in E♭ major. Both the descending triad formed by the first three notes and the ascending arpeggios leading to the top note in bar 5 suggest C minor, while the intervening notes blur any sense of E♭ major with a blue note that could either be the the flat 3rd of E♭ or the flat 5th of C minor – the common blues vocal inflection mentioned on page 70.

The second phrase doesn't dispel this tonal uncertainty, for now there is more chromaticism, the darker sound of the minor 7th (D♭) appears and the repeated use of G♭ hints at E♭ minor. Armstrong establishes a four-note motif that outlines an E♭ minor triad in bar seven and then develops this idea sequentially in bar eight (outlining a B♭ minor chord) and inverts it in bar nine. He continues the downward movement with a twisting and turning phrase implying the chords of F minor (bar ten) and B♭^{7} (bar 11). This II–V progression, whose cadential function will be familiar from your study of tonality in classical music, expectantly sets up the entrance of the band on an augmented dominant chord and thus leads smoothly into the E♭ major blues.

E♭m   B♭m   Fm   B♭^{7} B♭+
E♭ major: II   V^7 V$^{aug.\,5}$

> **Warning.** Photocopying any part of this book without permission is illegal.

Armstrong is similarly creative in terms of rhythm. He establishes a fast pulse with crotchets then increases the sense of movement with triplet crotchets. After a brief but dramatic pause on the top note he goes up another gear with quavers and triplet quavers in the remaining bars. To some extent the way in which Armstrong expands and contracts rhythmic values in a declamatory, speech-like manner defies notation, but the general principle of increasing momentum is clearly evident.

Louis Armstrong's sound is full and warm, with fast vibrato and versatile articulation. His staccato tonguing gradually becomes more legato as the pace of the introduction increases. Notice how he swells on the triplet quavers in the second phrase to give them momentum and the way he introduces a fast vibrato at the end of the held notes which complete each phrase. The passage shows how Armstrong established new technical standards for all trumpeters, particularly in extending the upper range of the instrument.

Chorus 1   0:17

The head consists of a slow 12-bar blues trumpet theme, starting with the F#–G–B♭ pattern that Armstrong had hinted at in bars 1–2 of the introduction. He begins with simple stately phrases and gradually raises the tension with dissonant notes (notice bar 5), chromatic notes and increasingly shorter note values, just as he did in the intro. The rising triplet arpeggio idea which concludes the chorus is closely related to the first phrase of the introduction, and helps to unify the performance.

Expressive instrumental techniques

There are some interesting examples of trumpet techniques in this first chorus. The dip in pitch on the long B♭ in bar 5 is achieved by 'lipping' the note down with the embouchure, and is known as a **scoop**. In bar nine Armstrong 'swallows' the A♭. Listen carefully and notice how the quiet A♭ barely has a beginning or end, and how it contrasts with the assertive C that follows. There is constant use of vibrato at the *end* of longer notes, an effect that has been termed 'terminal vibrato'. Finally on the high B♭ which concludes the chorus, Armstrong uses a **lip trill** (made by using the lips, not the valves) to decorate the B♭ with a fast trill to the C above.

The trombone and clarinet accompany, mainly with long notes which outline the changes in harmony but keep clear of the busy solo line, while piano and banjo play clipped chords on the beat. Notice how the trombonist uses the slide to smear the pitches.

Chorus 2   0:52

Fred Robinson's trombone solo offers a strong contrast to the first chorus, achieved through the economic use of fewer pitches and longer note-lengths, the plaintive quality of the high register of the trombone and the extensive portamento resulting from use of the slide. His choice of notes is closely linked with Earl Hines' tremolo piano chords. The top line of these chord voicings (the highest note

The word tessitura refers to the part of the pitch range in which the music mainly lies.

of each chord) forms a countermelody which moves at a similar pace to the solo and occupies the same tessitura as the trombone.

Notice the curious way in which the sad quality of the trombone solo is accompanied by the rather jolly chomping of a percussion device known as the *bock-a-da-bock*. This consists of two metal discs (each about three inches in diameter) mounted on sprung tongs, which the drummer cups in his hands to play.

1:26 Chorus 3 This takes the form of a call-and-response duet between clarinet and voice, accompanied by comping from piano and banjo. Jimmy Strong uses the low (chalumeau) register of the clarinet and employs a fast vibrato typical of New Orleans clarinettists. During the long notes his phrases are at first imitated and then answered by Armstrong in a jazz singing style that he is credited with inventing, known as **scat** (singing to improvised nonsense syllables). Notice the expressive use of an appoggiatura D against the prevailing E♭ harmony in bar 2 (marked * in the example, *left*) and bar 8. Armstrong's fluent vocal responses in this chorus bear a close resemblance to his trumpet style. In the last two bars, clarinet and vocals descend chromatically together in 3rds.

2:00 Chorus 4 An unaccompanied piano solo by Earl Hines provides another change in texture. Bars 1–4 and 9–12 consist of delicately executed arpeggiation in right hand, covering a wide range. In contrast the middle four bars use a more percussive and syncopated line in octaves, ending with a tremolo. The left hand uses a style known as 'stride piano' that derives from ragtime, with wide leaps between bass and harmony notes.

2:34 Chorus 5 and coda The entire frontline returns for this climactic final chorus, in which Armstrong starts the theme an octave higher and then holds the high B♭ for four bars before descending with a cascade of notes as the band resolves the tension of E♭^{7} harmony onto a chord of A♭. He again recycles material from the introduction, this time the descending E♭ minor triad idea, but delivers it in such a dramatic and arresting fashion that it sounds fresh and new. He then builds up to an impassioned 'rip' between the G and B♭ in bar 8, which is achieved by tightening the embouchure and using false fingerings.

The accompaniment for this astonishing passage varies little from the pattern of sustained notes and comping established in the first four bars, although it is worth noting how the clarinettist picks up the appoggiatura from the third chorus to use for a final expressive gesture in bar 8 (see *above*). Armstrong's trumpet seems to float over all this, freely negotiating restrictions of metre and tonality. After he comes to rest a brief piano solo leads to the short coda. Here a gradually slowing trumpet solo based on a pentatonic scale cues the other frontline players to join for the last three held chords. The closing of the cymbal tongs brings proceedings to an end.

Private study

1. What are the differences between the two parts of Armstrong's solo introduction?
2. Name four techniques used by Louis Armstrong to enhance the expressive quality of his sound in the first chorus.
3. Explain the meaning of 'portamento' and 'stride piano', and give an example of the use of each in *West End Blues*.
4. How does the second chorus differ from the first?

Group work

If someone in your group plays a wind instrument, see how many different ways they can change the sound by experimenting with pitch and articulation. In particular try searching for the notes between the semitones. Can any of these techniques be adapted to string instruments and piano? If you have access to a synthesizer, can you emulate effects such as pitch bend convincingly?

Listen to *West End Blues* and then discuss the following points:

✦ The 12-bar blues can be a very sectionalised form. How are the intro and choruses joined to make the piece more cohesive?
✦ Which common rhythm-section instrument is missing from this early recording? Can you suggest a reason why it wasn't used?
✦ *West End Blues* ends with a highly chromatic version of which standard type of cadence?

Composing

If you are opting to arrange a lead sheet for Section B of the composing unit, a traditional blues would be a good choice, as you could start with just a couple of choruses as a practice exercise and then extend it later once you are satisfied with the results. There are plenty from which to choose, including others recorded by Armstrong that would serve as models, such as *Melancholy Blues* and the famous *St Louis Blues*.

Study the construction and development of Armstrong's ideas, particularly his use of decreasing note lengths to heighten tension. Use melodic devices such as blue notes, **enclosures** and chromatic approach notes. Then play your chorus against a simple comping pattern set up on a sequencer or played on a piano. Try decorating the solo with some timbral effects. Then write a second chorus for two soloists in dialogue, like the third chorus of *West End Blues*.

Selected discography

Louis Armstrong: Hot Fives and Hot Sevens Volume 3. *JSP CD314*. *West End Blues* also features on many other CD compilations, but make sure the one you use is a copy of the original 1928 recording and not a performance that Armstrong recorded later in his life.

Louis Armstrong and King Oliver's Creole Jazz Band. *Tradition TCD1069*. This illustrates the collective style of early New Orleans music when Armstrong played second cornet to Oliver's lead.

Be aware that the word 'blues' appears in the title of some pieces, such as *Basin St Blues* and *Wild Man Blues*, that are not based on 12-bar blues sequences at all.

An **enclosure** is a term used in jazz for the device of approaching a main note from pitches on either side (above and below), as in the approach to G and B♭ in bars 7–8 of the trumpet solo in the first chorus:

At the time of going to press OCR was planning to issue its own CD of the prescribed jazz works to include the specified version of this piece.

Further listening

Further reading

Early Jazz by Gunther Schuller. *Oxford University Press*, 1968/1986. ISBN: 0-19-504043-0. This has an excellent chapter on Armstrong with detailed analysis of his style and extensive transcriptions.

Aural practice

This extract will be found between timings 0:52 and 1:25 on the CD. If your CD player has A–B repeat mode you could loop this section for convenience.

This skeleton score shows parts of the trombone solo and bass line in the second chorus of *West End Blues*. Listen to this section of the CD as many times as you need while answering the questions below.

1. What playing technique does the trombonist use at the start? ....
2. Identify the chord marked **X** in bar 2. ....
3. Compare the chords in bars 5 and 6. ....
4. Add the correct rhythm to the trombone pitches shown in bar 5 and the first two beats of bar 6.
5. Complete the bass-clef trombone melody in bars 8–9 (the rhythm to use is given below the stave).
6. Complete the bass part in bars 10–11 using a rhythm of four crotchets in each bar.
7. What playing technique is used by the pianist in this extract? ....

Question practice

1. Explain the significance of Louis Armstrong's contribution to the development of jazz.
2. Briefly describe the variety of different instrumental textures used in *West End Blues*.
3. Describe four instrumental techniques commonly used in jazz to enhance musical expression that would not be used when playing orchestral works by Haydn or Mozart.
4. How is it possible to include some variety in tonality when improvising a blues?

Warning. Photocopying any part of this book without permission is illegal.

Rockin' In Rhythm   Duke Ellington (1931)

Prescribed for examination in 2003 and 2004

Duke Ellington (1899–1974) is unique in the history of jazz as the only major figure whose importance arises more from skill as a composer than from performing and improvising. Ellington was a more than adequate pianist, but his reputation is due to the quality of his compositions, his idiosyncratic arranging style and his expertise as a bandleader in moulding the individual talents of his musicians into a balanced whole. Indeed it has been said that the orchestra itself was Ellington's instrument. He was extremely prolific and produced over 1,000 pieces, ranging from nightclub floorshow numbers to film scores and church music. It is thus not possible to pigeon-hole his work under one style or era of jazz – Ellington's music is really a category unto itself. He remains the most important and influential composer in the history of jazz.

Unlike Louis Armstrong's roots in the poor south of the USA, Ellington was born into a middle class family in a northern city, Washington D.C. His early musical experiences were of playing commercial music for society parties and embassy functions, and he spent some time in New York in the early 1920s playing and writing Broadway shows. It was while in New York that he heard and was influenced by the ragtime and stride playing of Harlem pianists Willie 'The Lion' Smith and James P. Johnson.

While in New York he played in a band called the Washingtonians with some of the musicians who would go on to form the nucleus of his own band, including Arthur Whetsol, 'Tricky Sam' Nanton and Harry Carney (see box, *right*). Ellington eventually took over leadership of the band and secured a four-year residency at the Cotton Club in Harlem from 1927 to 1931. Here he developed what became known as his 'jungle' style to accompany the stylised floorshows presented nightly to all-white audiences. These pieces are characterised by dark, brooding saxophone textures that form a backdrop for the raw growling of the brass soloists, who used various combinations of mutes and extended instrumental techniques to create rough, vibrant sounds.

The long engagement at the Cotton Club enabled Ellington to pursue an interest in programme music and exotica, which distinguished his band from the more functional dance music bands of the era. His compositional style was also strongly influenced by the playing of his band members, many of whom stayed with him for decades. He incorporated their individual abilities into his writing, in a symbiotic relationship in which the players' musical personalities and sounds fed into the character of the piece and they in turn were nourished by the creation of a sympathetic context in which to practise their art. This became known as 'the Ellington effect'.

Rockin' In Rhythm was recorded in 1931, just before the end of the Cotton Club stint that had made the band extremely famous, not least because of the many national radio broadcasts that they made during their tenure. At this point the Ellington band was about to embark on a life of constant international touring and recording that was to remain the pattern until the bandleader's death over 40 years later.

Rockin' In Rhythm

Composed by Duke Ellington and Harry Carney (arranged Ellington) Recorded 14 January 1931 in New York by Duke Ellington and his Orchestra.

Trumpets: Cootie Williams
            Arthur Whetsol
            Freddy Jenkins
Trombone: Joe 'Tricky Sam' Nanton
Clarinet /
Tenor sax: Barney Bigard
Alto saxes: Johnny Hodges
            Harry Carney
Piano: Duke Ellington
Banjo: Fred Guy
Bass: Wellman Braud
Drums: Sonny Greer

Warning. Photocopying any part of this book without permission is illegal.

Listening guide

| Time | 0:00 | **Intro** |

Ellington's piano introduction begins on a remote B^7 chord, but quickly works its way around the circle of 5ths to C with a driving, syncopated figure. The home key is emphasised by the descending scalic line from tonic to dominant on trombone and bass:

Form

	Intro	4 bars
A	Theme	26 bars
A^3	Trumpet solo	16 bars
A	Theme + link	30 bars
B	Clarinet solo	16 bars
	Intro repeated	4 bars
A^3	Trombone solo	16 bars
A	Theme	26 bars

| 0:05 | **A** |
| | **Theme** |

The theme consists of three eight-bar sections, each using the same chord pattern, plus a two-bar extension. This chord pattern underpins most of the piece (thematic variants are identified below as A^1, A^2 and A^3). Note the extremely pianistic voicing of the close-harmony reeds. The lively saxophone writing is parallel throughout the piece and uses both diatonic and chromatic passing chords (see bars 5 and 8 respectively). The high tessitura of the reeds gives a bright, well-projected sound. Piano and banjo chords are accented on beats two and four in response to the 'two-in-a-bar' feel of the bass, which rises against the descending contour of the melody in bars 5–7:

A^1 These four bars are repeated with a varied ending that leads to the second section based on the same chord pattern. Variation in the frontline writing is created by more sustained parts for reeds. The pitches of the descending saxophone melody (*left*) are drawn from the consonant sound of the major pentatonic scale, to which a solo trumpet responds with a bluesy E♭ on the way down to the tonic.

A^2 In the final eight-bar section the reeds return to a more punchy, syncopated line derived from bar 7 above. Their four-note rhythmic motif is answered each time by 'choked' hi-hat, a sound achieved by striking the cymbal and then immediately stopping the vibration by moving the two cymbals together with the foot pedal.

The seventh and eighth bars of this section use a descending scale idea, voiced in parallel triads. Ellington adds two extra bars (a 'tag') to the eight-bar section in order to extend the scale by an octave.

| 0:39 | **A^3** |
| | **Trumpet solo** |

The bass and comping instruments continue with the pattern used previously but the reeds have another new idea, related to their arpeggiated figures in A and A^2. However, this time their funky, off-beat **riff** is down an octave to create space for the trumpet solo. This sort of rolling, mid-range saxophone figure was to become a stock Ellington device in years to come. Notice that the melodic lines of A and A^1 are four-bar units, while A^2 and A^3 use repeated one-bar and two-bar ideas to give a sense of movement and development over what is virtually an identical background arrangement.

A **riff** is a short melodic idea which repeats many times, often remaining unaltered in pitch when the harmony changes.

Warning. Photocopying any part of this book without permission is illegal.

The trumpet line itself is very regular and measured; it is hard to say whether this is an improvised solo that Cootie Williams refined over the many times he performed it, or whether it was a written solo which was freely interpreted. There was a tradition in this band of incorporating improvised lines into the arrangement, so that a new player coming into the band could play a paraphrased version of the solo recorded by the musician he replaced.

All 26 bars (A, A^1 and A^2) of the theme are restated, with just a small difference in the concluding two-bar tag, which Ellington adapts to suit a new scoring for brass. This leads into a four-bar **vamp** which, after so many repetitions of the A section sequence, provides a welcome contrast by establishing the darker tonality of A minor (the relative minor) as a new key centre.

The vamp continues as a backing for the clarinet solo, with the bass setting up a V–I ostinato and the banjo playing chord I on every beat. Ellington plays on the off-beats with a stress on the second beat of the bar in response to the strong first beat of the bass line (listen out for Ellington's accidental A-major chord). We can also hear a perky woodblock accompaniment from the drummer – and a bass-drum pattern which is so strictly on the beat that it is slightly at odds with the piano, which tends to anticipate these beats.

Like the trumpet solo it is hard to be sure of the precise origin of the clarinet solo, but the way that the melody repeats exactly after eight bars tells us that clearly this is predetermined material. The melody is extremely symmetrical in contour, with snaking chromatic runs leading up to high C in the first four bars, and then a gradual descent in the next four. This section may have been included to accompany some arabic scene in the floorshow.

From this point on there is no new material as such. The four-bar intro is repeated, leading into more repetitions of chord pattern A.

The next 16 bars feature an improvised solo for muted trombone. The accompaniment uses the same texture of reeds and rhythm section as the trumpet solo in A^3, the only difference being a more urgent performance by the rhythm section, who emphasise the accent at the end of the saxophone riff much more strongly. Because of the combination of muted trombone with the low voicing of the reeds, there is plenty of contrast between this section and the entire reprise of the theme that follows, in which the reeds suddenly spring up over an octave.

All three sections of the theme (A, A^1 and A^2) are repeated for a final time. At the end of the tag the descending scale figure is slowed to a halt and accompanied by a bugle-like rising 5th (from tonic to dominant) on the trumpet.

Rockin' In Rhythm is constructed from relatively little material – mainly two-, four- and eight-bar melodic ideas in parallel triadic harmony over a repeating eight-bar chord pattern. The use of the same backing for both the brass solos gives the work as a whole a type of arch form (A–A^3–A–B–A^3–A). Variety comes from:

✦ using progressively shorter melodic ideas to create a sense of urgency

Theme 0:59

A **vamp** is a repeated chord pattern played to prepare for the entry of a soloist. The number of repeats is not always fixed – the instruction 'vamp tlil ready' can allow time for preparation and some audience reaction to greet the soloist.

B 1:38
Clarinet solo

Because of technical difficulty in capturing the wide dynamic range of drums in early recordings, drummers often used novelty effects (such as the woodblock here or the cymbal tongs in *West End Blues*) rather than playing 'time' on the full drum kit.

Intro 1:58

A^3 2:03
Trombone solo

Theme 2:23

Warning. Photocopying any part of this book without permission is illegal.

- alternating sections that are dominated by reeds with those that feature brass solos
- contrasting descending melodies with ascending bass lines
- varying the rhythm section parts
- changing the tessitura of the reeds to create light and dark sounds
- having a central B section in which the key and mood changes.

Improvisation and instrumental technique

Trumpet The phrasing of Cootie Williams' trumpet solo is closely integrated with the saxophone backing, suggesting that it was written, or that he worked it out in advance. His exclusively descending melodic lines are almost completely diatonic and very clearly outline the essentially I–IV–I–VI–II–V progression of the cyclical chord pattern. This is very much a swing solo in its rhythmic language, with the consistent use of swing quavers and repetition of typical swing patterns. His sound is full and broad, and as was usual with brass players in New York-based bands he uses less vibrato than the New Orleans trumpet players of the time. His articulation is a mixture of firmly-tongued detached off-beat notes and slurred runs.

Clarinet Although coming from New Orleans, Barney Bigard plays his clarinet solo in a cleaner, less affected fashion than most other New Orleans clarinettists. Comparing this solo with the clarinet playing on Armstrong Hot Five or Hot Seven recordings of around the same period, one finds that Bigard uses the typical fast vibrato on his high Cs, and slides between some long notes, but much of the playing is relatively restrained.

Trombone The most spontaneous improvisation is by 'Tricky Sam' Nanton on trombone, but comparison with an earlier recording of this piece reveals that even this was planned to some extent. He bases almost the entire solo on rocking back and forth between the root and 5th (could this be in response to the title of the piece?) and the solo is entirely within the compass of an octave. Nanton doesn't coordinate with the saxophone figure in the way that Cootie Williams does but instead uses a great deal of accented syncopation that crosses the rhythmic patterns of the reeds. What is most remarkable is his sound, which is achieved by the use of a straight or 'pixie' mute. As well as exploiting the rough timbre produced by this mute when played at a high dynamic level, on some notes Nanton also 'growls' (literally growling with the vocal chords while playing the instrument) to make the sound rougher still. This is an example of the 'jungle' style of brass playing developed in the Ellington band.

Ensemble At the beginning of A^1, notice how the reeds scoop up to their long notes by bending the note with the embouchure and then gradually lifting it to its eventual pitch – listen to how they skillfully co-ordinate the speed and intensity of their vibrato at this point. Similarly listen out for the malleable, slippery nature of the reeds' backing at A^3. Piano, banjo and drums have a specific role to play in punctuating melodies with accented chords; this requires a wide dynamic range in order to emphasise the strong and weak beats. The drums are used in an almost orchestral way, with just one or two sounds at a time to decorate the music rather than to underpin it, perhaps due to the problems at this time of recording drum kits.

Private study

1. Why is Ellington unique among the leading figures of jazz?

2. What is meant by the 'Ellington effect'?

3. Why might *Rockin' In Rhythm* be described as an arch form?

4. In which sections do you hear the following?

    (i) a V–I ostinato
    (ii) a circle of 5ths
    (iii) elaboration of a basic I–IV–I–VI–II–V chord pattern.

5. In what way is the writing in this piece pianistic?

6. What techniques do the brass soloists employ to achieve the distinctive 'jungle' sound?

Group work

Listen carefully to the rhythm section throughout *Rockin' In Rhythm* and make brief notes on how their parts change during the course of the piece. One of the group should try to identify the only place in the work where all three trumpets play. Compare your notes.

Listening

If you can get hold of the version of *Rockin' In Rhythm* recorded by the jazz-fusion group Weather Report in 1980 make a comparison with the original version in terms of:
+ tempo
+ instrumentation and texture
+ form
+ mood and atmosphere
+ rhythmic feel.

This version is available on **Night Passage** by Weather Report, *CBS / Sony 8459*.

Which do you prefer and why?

Invent a simple vamp like the section B idea in *Rockin' In Rhythm* (see *right*). This could be looped on a sequencer or played on keyboard or guitar. Each take turns to improvise over this ostinato. Don't be afraid to start with the simplest ideas – just a repeated note in a syncopated pattern, if you like. Keep going for eight bars and make sure the next person starts without a gap.

Improvising

As you get more confident, attempt some limited melodic movement in contrary motion to the bass. Then try four bars from one of the group answered by four from the next person. In the answering phrases try to respond to what you hear, at first by echoing it exactly, then by varying it a little by adding your own ideas.

If this works well, try inventing a one-bar riff idea, with a slight change in the fourth bar, that fits with the vamp. Use two players on this, harmonising in thirds, or three players harmonising in parallel triads, like Ellington's reed parts. Once this is secure, reduce the dynamic so that this texture can be used as a backdrop for improvised solos.

Composing

If you are opting to arrange a lead-sheet for Section B of the composing unit you should have little difficulty in finding suitable

A lead-sheet for *Mood Indigo* can be found in volume 2 of *The New Real Book* (Sher Music Co). *Caravan* is in volume 3.

material from among Ellington's hundreds of compositions, should you wish to use one as a source. There is no need for your arrangement to follow the style of *Rockin' In Rhythm*, although there is much to be learnt from using Ellington as a model of good jazz arrangement and we have outlined a number of the techniques he uses. Possible melodies, dating from around this period, include *The Creole Love Call*, *It Don't Mean a Thing if It Ain't Got That Swing*, *Mood Indigo* and the ever-popular minor-key *Caravan*.

Further reading

Early Jazz by Gunther Schuller. *Oxford University Press*, 1968/1986. ISBN: 0-19-504043-0. This includes an excellent chapter on early Ellington, and although it doesn't look specifically at this piece, there is a detailed analysis of Ellington's influences and developing style, with historical context and extensive transcriptions.

Selected discography

At the time of going to press OCR was planning to issue its own CD of the prescribed jazz works to include the specified version of this piece.

The Best of Early Ellington. *Decca GRP 16602*. This CD includes the correct version of *Rockin' In Rhythm* for the OCR exam but it is currently no longer available. There are many compilations and other reissues which feature a version recorded a few days before this version. While this is similar it differs from the version to be studied in some important ways.

Further listening Listen to recordings by Louis Armstrong's Hot Fives and Hot Sevens (see page 77) to compare the New Orleans style being recorded in Chicago at this time with Ellington's New York orchestra.

Aural practice

This extract will be found between timings 2:03 and 2:22 on the CD. If your CD player has A–B repeat mode you could loop this section for convenience.

This skeleton score printed opposite shows parts of the trombone solo and bass part of *Rockin' In Rhythm*. Listen to this section of the CD as many times as you need while answering the questions below.

1. Complete the bass part in bar 2 by writing on the score the pitches of the four crotchets heard.

2. Identify the chord marked **X** in bar 3. ....

3. In bars 10 and 11 circle *three* beats on which you hear the bass play the tonic.

4. Complete the trombone part in bars 13–15. The rhythm to use is printed above the stave.

5. Write the symbols II–V⁷–I under the bass part below the notes where you hear this progression.

6. Describe the rhythm of the trombone solo in bars 6–8. ....

7. State *two* methods used by the soloist to modify the natural sound of the trombone.

   ....

8. Underline *one* of the following descriptions which best describes the trombone solo.

   chromatic   diatonic   based on a blues scale   based entirely on the tonic triad

9. Which of the descriptions in question 8 best describes the saxophone backing? ....

10. Briefly describe the part played by the rhythm section in this extract. ....

    ....

84 Rockin' In Rhythm

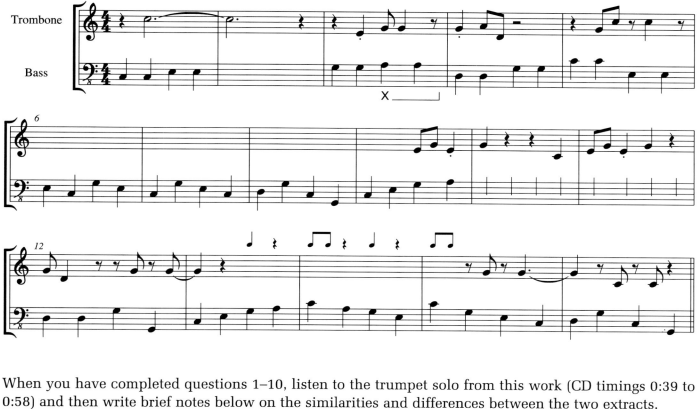

When you have completed questions 1–10, listen to the trumpet solo from this work (CD timings 0:39 to 0:58) and then write brief notes below on the similarities and differences between the two extracts.

....
....
....
....
....
....

Question practice

1. Explain the significance of Duke Ellington's contribution to the development of jazz.

2. *Rockin' In Rhythm* is dominated by the reed ensemble; what did Ellington do to create variation?

3. By 1931 jazz was one of the most successful types of popular music. How do you account for its appeal?

4. Compare two contrasting jazz solos, explaining the different approaches to improvisation of the two performers.

5. What is meant by Ellington's 'jungle' style?

6. Was the harmonic language of early jazz entirely new, or did it derive in part from classical music?

   TIP: Question 6 invites discussion of a range of issues. You will need to consider the types of chord employed, how those chords are used in progressions, ways in which they might be modified and the types of modulation typically used.

Warning. Photocopying any part of this book without permission is illegal.

Prescribed for examination in 2001 and 2002

Ko-ko   Duke Ellington (1940)

Before starting this chapter, read page 79 for an introduction to Ellington's early life and music. Also reread the section on page 68 about blues harmony.

By 1940 Duke Ellington's band was widely regarded as the most forward-looking and experimental popular big band in America. The swing craze that swept the USA during the 1930s had produced a great number of big bands playing swing (dance music influenced by jazz) and popular songs, often with a featured vocalist. But the Ellington band played a great deal of instrumental music, and the material was often adventurous and strikingly original. Ellington continued to develop the distinctive programmatic approach he adopted during the band's long residency at the Cotton Club at the end of the 1920s and tended to avoid the noisy and hectic 'flag wavers' that were the stock-in-trade of many conventional big bands. Instead there was a more finely balanced compositional aesthetic that encompassed some very exciting and vibrant dance music, but which avoided the clichés of the swing idiom. Ellington's band could also be distinguished from most other big bands by the number and quality of the soloists in its ranks, and the way in which the leader composed specific settings to complement the musical personality and character of each.

As a result of this more considered and refined approach, the Ellington band was nowhere near as popular and commercially successful as many other bands. Ellington's music was sometimes dismissed by critics as not being 'real' jazz, but on the contrary it can now be seen that Ellington was leading a general drift away from commercialisation. Jazz musicians began to regard their music as something other than the good-time party music it had been in the 1920s and early 1930s, and a division began to emerge between jazz-influenced dance music and jazz itself. Ellington was central to this process. By transforming the conventions of 'hot' music into something deeper and more lasting, and by integrating composition and improvisation, he moved jazz into a new area. This development was also encouraged by the way in which jazz was being treated as an art form by European intellectuals and critics, and the consequent reception that black American musicians enjoyed on their visits to Europe during the 1930s.

Composition and arrangement

The music of *Ko-ko* was originally written for an unperformed opera called *Boola*, sections of which Ellington later incorporated into his *Black, Brown and Beige Suite*. *Ko-ko* is widely regarded as one of his most creative and innovative works, despite the limit posed by the three-minute duration of the gramophone record of the time. By this stage many of Ellington's musicians had been working with him for some years (compare the list in the box on this page with that on page 79 and also note how the band had increased in size). Ellington's insight into ways to combine their particular sounds to achieve certain effects had increased, and there was a fluency and ease about the way in which the band performed his music.

Ko-ko

Composed and arranged by Duke Ellington. Recorded 6 March 1940 in Chicago by Duke Ellington and his Orchestra.

Trumpets:	Wallace Jones
	Cootie Williams
Cornet:	Rex Stewart
Trombones:	Lawrence Brown
	Joe Nanton
Valve trombone:	Juan Tizol
Clarinet:	Barney Bigard
Alto saxes:	Johnny Hodges
	Otto Hardwick
Tenor sax:	Ben Webster
Baritone sax:	Harry Carney
Piano:	Duke Ellington
Guitar:	Fred Guy
Double bass:	Jimmy Blanton
Drums:	Sonny Greer

Warning. Photocopying any part of this book without permission is illegal.

The piece consists of an eight-bar introduction, seven choruses of heavily-scored 12-bar blues in E♭ minor and a coda. The arrangement makes constant use of call-and-response patterns:

Form	Solo or unison line	Backing
Intro	Baritone sax	answered by trombones
Chorus 1	Valve trombone	answered by saxophones
Chorus 2	Muted trombone solo	reeds answered by brass
Chorus 3	(varied repeat of 2)	reeds answered by brass
Chorus 4	Piano solo	reeds answered by brass
Chorus 5	Trumpets in unison	reeds answered by trombones
Chorus 6	Reeds and brass	answered by solo bass
Chorus 7	Clarinet and brass	answered by saxophones
Coda	Extended version of intro	

The fact that it is a minor blues is significant. It was very unusual at the time for blues to be played in minor keys, but this innovation was to pass into common use during the 1950s and 1960s. *Ko-ko* is written in 'crescendo' form, an approach which Ellington had already experimented with in earlier works such as *Crescendo In Blue* (1937) and which was becoming increasingly popular with swing arrangers. However his use of the principle extends beyond dynamics and he gradually increases the intensity of the music by changing tessitura, harmonic density and rhythmic activity.

One of the most famous pieces based on a long crescendo and increasingly thickening textures to create tension during a repeated pattern is Ravel's *Bolero*, written in 1928. This work was well known in America, following Ravel's USA tour of 1928.

Listening guide

Much of the writing in *Ko-ko* derives directly from its opening bars, and consequently there are strongly related themes connecting the seven choruses. The baritone sax has a repeated pedal E♭ which is answered by trombones playing syncopated triads which descend chromatically. This establishes several ideas:

✦ an antiphonal call-and-response pattern
✦ a rhythmic motif of three swing quavers followed by a long note
✦ a solo from one section of the band contrasting with harmony from a different section.

Intro *Time* 0:00

This basic pattern is played four times in all, with the trombones beginning at a higher pitch in the second and third repetitions, before returning to their original starting notes. Tension is further intensified by the use of increasingly dissonant chords against the E♭ pedal. The thick sound of the low baritone sax, tom-toms and gruff trombones creates a dark and exotic opening, quite unlike the standard language of swing.

The theme is introduced on the valve trombone, an instrument equipped with trumpet-like valves instead of the usual slide. It has a thinner tone than the normal instrument, but is capable of fast passagework – the first two notes of the melody would require moving the slide to its full extent on a conventional tenor trombone, an impossible movement in the time available.

Chorus 1 0:12

The theme derives from the rhythm of the baritone sax in the intro (examples *a* and *b*, *left*). The saxophones answer the trombone in a direct reversal of the call-and-response format of the intro. The melody and the lead line of the saxophone responses use the natural minor scale (or aeolian mode), which is like the harmonic minor but without a sharpened leading note. This scale is the predominant source of melodic material throughout the piece, but the harmonisation is based on richly chromatic chords that are not at all modal.

For the first eight bars of the chorus the trombone and saxophones have a two-bar phrase played four times. In bars 9–10 this pattern is contracted, so that the trombone is answered in every bar, while bars 11–12 return to the original two-bar pattern. Ellington introduces a third element to the call-and-response pattern at this point with his off-beat dominant pedals. Note that the saxophones' phrase is transposed up a 4th when the harmony changes from chord I to chord IV, but the trombone solo remains at the same pitch, thus preserving its modal quality.

The rhythm section accompanies with chords on the beat played by guitar, a hi-hat 'time' pattern from the drummer and a strong walking-bass line from Jimmy Blanton, whose playing was another innovative aspect of the Ellington band of this period. In the New Orleans style bassists had tended to play just on beats 1 and 3, or to use repeated pitches in each half of the bar, as shown in the extract from *Rockin' In Rhythm* on page 85. Blanton had the technical ability and musical knowledge to be able to change his pitch on *every* beat, and he established a new standard of improvised bass lines which is still relevant today.

0:24 **Chorus 2** In the second chorus Ellington continues with a three part call-and-response arrangement:

- unison saxophones play a variant of the first chorus theme, which is given an unresolved quality by its long A♭ (example *c*)
- the brass answer with off-beat chords that are accented by use of plunger ('wah-wah') mutes – see page 90
- Ellington punctuates the end of the brass phrase with a percussive mid-range chord.

This texture, along with the comping of the rhythm section, acts as a vivid backdrop to Joe Nanton's fierce muted-trombone solo.

0:49 **Chorus 3** In the third chorus the frontline arrangement remains the same for the first eight bars, and is only slightly altered in the last four. The trombone solo moves up in register and dynamic.

1:07 **Chorus 4** Ellington maintains many of the elements from the previous two choruses. There is continued unison writing for saxes, played more strongly but employing the same four-note motif (example *d*), and the brass have more off-beat chords but with a higher voicing and a shorter rhythmic pattern. The rhythm section maintain the same steady role throughout. However, this continuity contrasts strongly with Ellington's dissonant **bitonal** interjections on piano.

Bitonality is the use of two keys at the same time.

The three principal motifs established so far end on E♭, A♭ and D♭ (examples *b*, *c* and *d*). These long sustained notes bring a new harmonic dimension to the 12-bar chord sequence on each of its

Warning. Photocopying any part of this book without permission is illegal.

repeats. E♭–A♭–D♭ suggests II–V–I movement towards D♭ major, and starts to undermine the strong E♭ minor that began the piece, introducing a sense of tonal ambiguity by the time we reach the optimistic-sounding D♭ in this fourth chorus.

The following three choruses suggest a similar pattern of F–B♭–E♭, thus closing the circle and bringing the music to the home key.

Chorus 5 1:25

Ellington starts to build intensity in a variety of ways. The trumpets take over the four-note unison motif (example *e*), playing in the weighty middle range of the instrument. They are answered by reeds and trombones. The widely spaced saxophones, led by a high clarinet, play a sustained chord. This in turn is answered by low trombones and baritone playing a dense voicing decorated by an inverted mordent. The tangible increase in tension is generated by:

- widely-spaced voicings which employ the extremities of each instrument's range
- use of the trumpets to play the theme
- a rise in the dynamic level
- an increase in rhythmic activity.

Chorus 6 1:43

This chorus offers a brief respite from the relentless momentum generated so far. Ellington builds a towering chord by staggering the entries of the reeds, trombones and trumpets, each of which then holds the final note of the four-note motif (see example *f*). This jazz-arranging technique is known as a 'pyramid' chord. The forceful sound is answered by solo bass playing a walking line. This four-bar pattern is played three times, varied by the use of a rising and falling trumpet line in the middle four bars, and by the reversal of trombone and trumpet entries in the last four bars.

Chorus 7 2:01

The final chorus is of a type known as a 'shout chorus' by jazz arrangers, due to its climactic ensemble writing. Ellington scores the clarinet and brass in widely-spaced held chords which provide the vivid backdrop for a descending unison saxophone melody that is a developed version of the first-chorus saxophone response:

In bars 9–10 of the chorus Ellington breaks the two-bar rhythmic pattern established in the first eight bars, and increases dissonance by use of the flattened 5th of the dominant chord – a discord that is reflected in the brass voicing. He retains the essence of the question-and-answer format, beginning block chords before the barline (an 'anticipation') and starting each saxophone phrase on the quaver after the downbeat (a 'delay'). This contraction of space between question and answer also adds to the momentum.

Coda 2:20

This starts with an exact repeat of the intro, which dies away with a decrescendo in bars 7–8. Then, in four final bars which follow, the trombones try to continue the rhythmic pattern of the intro but are quickly engulfed by rising chords from the trumpets and then the saxes, using the four-note 'pyramid' idea from the sixth chorus. Also notice the increased activity from the bass and drums, who begin playing quavers in the ninth bar and this introduces the rhythm taken up by the reeds in the next bar.

> Warning. Photocopying any part of this book without permission is illegal.

Summary

Ko-ko is representative of Ellington's mature work and contains elements that led to the modern jazz styles of the late 1940s:

- there are no tunes as such – it is based on motivic development
- it is not organised in the usual head–solos–head format
- it uses complex, densely-voiced chords and chromaticism
- it features an innovative and influential walking-bass style
- it is not written for dancing and is closer in its aesthetic to art music than the commercial music of its day.

Improvisation and instrumental technique

Plunger mutes

During the 1930s and 1940s, the Ellington band was immediately recognisable by the sound of its brass soloists, who developed a rough and vibrant tone by a combination of mutes and effects. In his *Ko-ko* solo, Joe Nanton attaches a straight mute to the bell of the trombone and then uses a plunger (the rubber suction cup from a plumber's plunger) to produce the characteristic 'wah-wah' effect.

Ellington also specifies the use of plunger mutes in written brass parts, such as in the backings in the second and third choruses. Here the brass alternate a 'closed' sound where the plunger is held close to the bell to suppress the note, with 'open' notes where the mute is held away from the bell. Moving from one to the other has a significant effect on dynamics, with the open notes being much louder and more accented than the closed notes.

Trombone solo (choruses 2 and 3)

Joe Nanton brings an urgency and directness to his solo by keeping to the top octave of the trombone range. In chorus 2 his playing is centred around the fourth and fifth of the key, and repeatedly uses the same melodic and rhythmic shape in classic blues fashion. In the next chorus he maintains these phrasing patterns but moves the idea up in pitch, reaching toward the flattened seventh of the key. At the same time he increases intensity by playing louder but closing the plunger to create a compellingly dramatic ending. Nanton uses both the mute and the slide to achieve microtonal inflections of pitch, and often ends phrases by 'falling' off the last note, achieved by careful coordination of embouchure and slide.

Notice that Nanton's solo has very little melodic material and that he tends to repeat his rhythmic ideas. He is more concerned with sound and timbre, and his solo is a connecting strand between the brass chords and the saxophone line; he uses the sound of the former and the pitches of the latter.

Private study

Check your understanding of this chapter by answering each of the following questions.

1. How was the music played by Ellington's band different to that played by the popular swing bands of the time?
2. What is unusual about the form of *Ko-ko*?
3. In what respect is *Ko-ko* modal and in what respect is it not?
4. Explain the meaning of each of the following four terms: walking bass, bitonality, pyramid chord, plunger mute.

Group work

Listening

Listen several times to Ellington's piano solo in chorus 4 (1:07 to 1:24) and make notes on exactly what you hear. Compare notes with the rest of the group and then individually write a detailed description of this passage, using the style of the section on the trombone solo (page 90) as a guide. Mention how the three four-bar sections of the piano solo relate to each other and to the backing. Try to include most of the following words in your description: off-beat, angular, dissonant, bitonal, chords, scales, inversion.

Improvising

Set up a blues chord sequence in A minor, using the chord chart on page 68, to be played by a pianist or rhythm section, or recorded on a sequencer. Try improvising a motif of just four notes taken from the aeolian mode (the notes A–G with no sharps or flats) over the top of this. Be sparing in your ideas – aim for a rhythm that has plenty of rests or long notes and try to repeat that same rhythm every two bars. See if you can devise a motif that will fit over the whole sequence without changing pitch, like chorus 1 of *Ko-ko*. Others should then add a response to this motif. It could just be a single chord repeated a couple of times in a rhythmic style, but the chord itself must change to fit the chord sequence. In bars 9–10 make the call and the response happen within one bar, rather than two and then go back to the original pattern for the last two bars. Try to include a walking bass for double bass, cello or synth.

Composing

Arranging a lead-sheet in the style that Duke Ellington used at this time needs a secure grasp of complex harmony. Some of the simpler features are outlined in the paragraph above, but you would also need to experiment with other techniques, such as the sound of triads moving chromatically in parallel over a pedal note. Try them in different inversions and link up chains of chords by changing two notes and keeping one common note. Remember the importance of the constant contrasting timbres in *Ko-ko*. Well-known pieces played by Ellington at this time and found in many collections of lead-sheets, include *Chelsea Bridge*, *I Got It Bad* and the song Ellington adopted as his signature tune, *Take the 'A' Train*.

Further reading

Duke Ellington, Jazz Composer by Ken Rattenbury. *Yale University Press*, 1993. ISBN: 0-300-05507-2. This contains a full transcription of *Ko-ko* with analysis of Ellington's writing and arranging, and it deals in depth with other pieces from Ellington's mature period.

Selected discography

The Classic Tracks of the 1940s, Duke Ellington. *KAZ CD 308*. This is the CD specified by OCR but it may prove difficult to locate. There are many other compilations which include this track, but make sure the one you use has the original 1940 recording and not a different arrangement that Ellington recorded later in his life.

Essential Masters of Jazz, Count Basie. *Proper EMCD15*. Compare the Ellington band with the Count Basie orchestra, and listen for differences in the way the music is organised.

At the time of going to press OCR was planning to issue its own CD of the prescribed jazz works to include the specified version of this piece.

Warning. Photocopying any part of this book without permission is illegal.

Aural practice

This extract will be found between timings 0:24 and 0:42 on the CD.

The skeleton score printed below shows parts of the trombone solo and bass part of chorus 2 and the first few bars of chorus 3 from *Ko-ko*. Listen to this music as many times as you need while you answer the questions which follow.

1. What does the bass play in bars 2 and 3? ....
2. The reeds play the same long note in all the odd-numbered bars. On what pitch is this note? ....
3. Complete the trombone part in bars 5–6. The rhythm to use is printed above the stave.
4. Describe the rhythm of the two-bar brass riff heard throughout this extract. ....
5. What is unusual about this 12-bar blues chord sequence? ....
6. State *two* methods used by the soloist to modify the natural sound of the trombone.
    (i) in bars 1–12: ....
    (ii) from bar 13 onwards: ....

Question practice

1. Describe some of the many different contrasts of texture that Ellington achieves in his instrumentation of *Ko-ko*.
2. Compare Beethoven's use of brass instruments in the finale of his fifth symphony with Ellington's brass writing in *Ko-ko*.
3. Most of the instrumental writing in *Ko-ko* centres on developing short motifs rather than presenting tunes. To what extent is this true of the orchestral works you have studied for this unit?

Attempt this question only if you are taking the exam in 2001:

4. Compare Ellington's use of 'crescendo form' as a way to increase intensity in the scoring with Rossini's use of the crescendo.

Warning. Photocopying any part of this book without permission is illegal.

Move   Miles Davis (1949)

Prescribed for examination in 2003 and 2004

Trumpeter and composer Miles Davis (1926–91) was a hugely influential figure in the development of jazz. He established several new trends that became distinct styles in their own right, including modal jazz, jazz-rock fusion and cool jazz. The last of these was a direct outcome of the body of work from which *Move* is taken. The impact of these recordings is all the more significant for the fact that Davis was only 21 at the time of the first sessions, and the other main contributors were of a similar age.

Bebop

At the age of 18, while studying at the Juilliard School of Music in New York, Davis began going to jam sessions and 'after hours' clubs where a new style of jazz was being created by musicians such as Charlie Parker, Dizzy Gillespie and Thelonious Monk. This style, which became known as 'bebop', was played in small groups and was a reaction to the formulaic and predictable music that big-band swing had become during the early 1940s. Bebop musicians saw their music as a serious art form, played for listening rather than dancing. Bebop was constructed from:

- complex harmonic patterns utilising rich chords that had many alterations and extensions
- chromatic and highly decorated melodic lines, often using wide intervals and many sudden changes of direction
- fast tempi and driving rhythms which demanded virtuosic instrumental technique and musicianship.

Miles Davis abandoned his course at Juilliard to study informally with Parker and Gillespie. He was one of the few trumpet players initiated into this new language and was asked to join Parker's band when Gillespie was unavailable in 1945. Davis was 19 years old. This experience had a huge influence on him, but Davis was not naturally suited to the rigours of bebop trumpet playing. Gillespie had established fast, extremely high upper-register playing as the norm, but Davis preferred solos in the middle range of the trumpet with soft, legato articulation, influenced by the lyrical melodic style of people like tenor saxophonist Lester Young.

Before long he was looking for a new setting in which to present his playing, and he met an arranger called Gil Evans who had been writing for the Claude Thornhill band. In this band was an alto saxophonist called Lee Konitz and a baritone-sax player called Gerry Mulligan. All four were very keen on the sound made by the Thornhill band and set about organising a smaller group that could reproduce these sorts of textures and sounds. The result was the **Miles Davis Nonet** which had a standard rhythm section of piano, bass and drums but a frontline that included tuba, baritone sax and french horn as well as the more common trumpet, alto sax and trombone. Their unusual arrangements were by Evans, Mulligan and John Lewis, a classical and jazz pianist who had been a member of Gillespie's band and who later formed the Modern Jazz Quartet.

See page 106 for more information about the Claude Thornhill band.

The music written for the nonet is an unconventional mix of different elements. The legacy of the Thornhill band gives a light airy sound, smooth contours and little use of extremes of range or

Warning. Photocopying any part of this book without permission is illegal.

0:35	**Chorus 2** **Trumpet solo**	The second chorus consists of a 32-bar trumpet improvisation from Miles Davis, based on the changes. There are no arranged events as such in either this or the alto saxophone solo that comes next. Effectively what we hear is a band within a band; the entire frontline drops out except for the soloist, and the pianist enters to take over the accompaniment role. The resulting quartet of soloist, piano, bass and drums is typical of bebop for small groups.
1:02	**Chorus 3** **Alto sax solo**	The 32-bar AABA format is heard again in Lee Konitz's alto sax solo, but the intensity drops as the drummer switches from ride cymbal to hi-hat. He returns to ride cymbal in the last few bars to lead into the next section.
1:29	**Chorus 4** **Drum solo**	Instead of the usual statement and repeat of an eight-bar A section Lewis arranges the 16 bars into four four-bar units. In each of these the ensemble plays for two bars and the drummer responds with a two-bar break. The ensemble sections, which are shown *left*, can be characterised as follows:

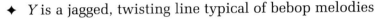

- X rises chromatically
- Y is a jagged, twisting line typical of bebop melodies
- X is then repeated
- Z features an inverted pedal (i.e. the pedal note is in the top part, not the bass) and continues into the drum break itself.

The beginning of the bridge is marked by the frontline players 'falling off' from a unison B♭ – a common big-band device. Max Roach then improvises alone for the remainder of the B section.

In the final eight bars of the drum chorus Lewis doesn't repeat the A section exactly. Instead he adds further interest by using Z first, and then Y, bringing a sense of reverse motion to the chorus.

1:56	**Chorus 5** **Theme**	The arranger creates interest in this reprise by varying the theme itself and by using different scoring for the accompaniment. There is far greater use of homophonic textures and less contrapuntal writing. The first A sections use block chords in the first two bars then a static chordal accompaniment for two bars. The following four bars have imitation of the melodic line in the tuba and baritone sax, and then a return to the homophonic texture.
		The bridge again features more parallel voicing of the melody and is much more uniform and symmetrical than the first chorus bridge with its cross rhythms. The A section repeats as usual, but this time the last two bars leads into the coda.
2:25	**Coda**	This consists of a series of dense chords unrelated to the key centre over which Davis improvises a fast moving quaver-based line. The baritone sax abruptly brings proceedings to a close with a sudden low F–B♭.

Improvisation and instrumental technique

The Miles Davis Nonet adopted a cleaner and purer approach to tone production and articulation than many of their contemporaries. This is evident in the sound of the trumpet and alto saxophone soloists.

Warning. Photocopying any part of this book without permission is illegal.

Miles Davis begins his trumpet solo with short phrases framed by the use of space. Several of the long notes are approached with a 'crushed note' on the semitone below. There are also some mis-pitched notes, probably arising from embouchure fatigue after playing the long and relentless theme. He then starts to adopt a more chromatic bebop-influenced style in which he fills in the gaps between diatonic notes. In the second A section this chromatic passagework starts to develop into longer phrases.

The strongly dissonant trumpet notes at the start of the bridge are supported by the pianist's chord voicing, suggesting that they may have agreed this passage in advance. The remainder of the bridge is taken up by a long phrase which spills over into the next A section. It consists almost exclusively of jazz quavers in small intervals, many of which form enclosures (see page 77). In this long phrase Miles uses a pattern of descending notes for one bar and ascending notes in the next. This is first repeated exactly and then freely varied. After this long phrase a short final idea ends on the dominant, ready for the immediate entry of the sax solo.

Lee Konitz's playing has none of the bending of pitches or vocalisation found in most jazz saxophonists of the time. Notice how clearly his sound emerges at the start of the solo, as the drummer switches to hi-hat and the pianist drops dramatically in dynamic, ready to build up during the next eight bars. Konitz immediately picks up on the momentum of the trumpet solo, but he differs from Davis in his phrase lengths and extensive use of the diatonic scale:

The following phrase is also seven bars long, exclusively diatonic and mainly scalic. However, Konitz varies his playing in the bridge by using four-bar phrases, the chromatic passing note technique that Davis had employed so extensively, and a brief hint at the 'secondary rag' rhythm of three-beat groupings in 4/4 time. There are also some very dissonant clashes against the underlying harmonies. The last A section has a release of all this tension by returning to diatonic material. The last four bars gather momentum as they run on into the beginning of the exchange between ensemble and drums.

Max Roach is well known for his 'melodic' drum solos. In his solo chorus he concentrates mainly on snare drum and tom-toms. Cymbal splashes at the ends of his solo phrases link into the ride cymbal time-playing that accompanies the next ensemble phrase. The first three responses are self-contained units with a moment's daylight between the end of the break and the entry of the ensemble. In the fourth break Roach plays across the formal division and into the middle eight, much in the way that Davis did in his solo.

The bridge gives the opportunity for a more extended break. It consists of four two-bar phrases, in which Roach establishes an idea and then varies it. He then repeats this process with a fresh idea. The first drum phrase of the final eight bars has a new off-beat feel to it, with a possible reference to the rhythmic language of Afro-Cuban music, but the last phrase is unequivocal in cueing in the band for the last head.

Trumpet

See the skeleton score on page 99 for an outline of this passage.

Alto saxophone

Drums

Warning. Photocopying any part of this book without permission is illegal.

Private study

1. What features of bebop can be found in *Move*? What other type of music influenced this piece?
2. What is unusual about the changes in *Move*?
3. Explain how the introduction is linked with the theme.
4. What is meant by the description of the drum solo as 'melodic'?
5. How does the last chorus differ from the first?

Group work

Improvising

Stand in a circle and establish a medium tempo with one person lightly clapping the pulse and everyone moving from foot to foot in time. Clap a one-bar pattern and leave three bars' rest. Repeat this four-bar unit, this time with the next person adding a one-bar pattern in the second bar. Continue in this way until the space is filled and all the separate parts are linked. Then start to add a few extra claps to the pattern so that the parts start to overlap. Transfer to instruments and do the same thing, using only a few pitches from a pentatonic scale. Starting from this base, improvise a piece constructed from interlocking rhythms. Remember that *when* you play is more important than what you play.

Composing

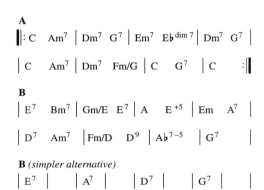

Try using some of John Lewis' techniques in your own arrangement of a song in 32-bar AABA form. You could write your own 'rhythm changes' tune if you wish (the basic chord sequence in C is shown *left*). Use a combination of syncopated triadic ideas and flowing scalic lines. Then write a countermelody that moves in the places that your first melody is static or silent and add a short riff that appears every two bars, like the one in the first chorus of *Move*. Use different textures to make the repetitions of section A more interesting – short chords in cross-rhythm with the tune, sustained chords, counterpoint, instruments in unison or octaves, and so on. Include a chorus in which the ensemble plays a two-bar pattern to act as a trigger for a two-bar response from a soloist, and then develop this in the style of chorus 4 from *Move*.

Further reading

Miles Davis: The Definitive Biography by Ian Carr. *HarperCollins*, revised 1999. ISBN: 0-00-653026-5. This doesn't focus in detail on *Move* but it shows the range of Davis' work and the huge influence he had on jazz. It also includes a number of transcriptions.

Selected discography

The Birth of the Cool, Miles Davis. *Capitol 92862*. This is the album from which *Move* is taken. Try to hear some late 1940s bebop such as **Now's The Time** (*Verve 5397572*) by Charlie Parker, one of the originators of the style and an early mentor to Miles Davis. **The Best of Gerry Mulligan With Chet Baker** (*Capitol 95481*) illustrates the extremely popular 1950s West Coast cool jazz style that was inspired by *The Birth of the Cool* sessions.

At the time of going to press OCR was planning to issue its own CD of the prescribed jazz works to include the specified version of this piece.

Warning. Photocopying any part of this book without permission is illegal.

Aural practice

The skeleton score printed below shows parts of the trumpet solo from Chorus 2 of *Move*. Listen to this music as many times as you need while you answer the questions which follow.

This extract will be found between timings 0:35 and 0:49 on the CD.

1. What term best describes the rhythm of the entire bass part? ....
2. Describe the scale pattern played by the bass in bar 5. ....
3. Describe the sound of the trumpet on the first note of bar 3. ....
4. In each of bars 7 and 14, write six quavers to show the pitches played by the trumpet.
5. What type of scale is played by the trumpet in bar 10? ....
6. In each of bars 9 and 13, write four crotchets to show the pitches played by the bass.
7. In what key is this extract? ....

Question practice

1. Compare the style of jazz arrangement used in *Move* with Duke Ellington's style of arranging in *Rockin' In Rhythm*.
2. Give a brief account of Miles Davis' trumpet improvisation in *Move*, explaining how it achieves a sense of development as it goes on and how it relates to the underlying changes.
3. Why is Miles Davis regarded as such an important figure in the development of modern jazz?
4. Explain, in non-technical language suitable for the general listener, how *Move* is related to the two songs on which its harmonies are based.
5. In what ways did the newly developing technology of recording affect jazz?

Warning. Photocopying any part of this book without permission is illegal.

Prescribed for examination in 2001 and 2002

All Blues   Miles Davis (1959)

Before starting this chapter read pages 93–94 for a description of Miles Davis' early career and developments in modern jazz in the 1940s and 1950s.

The year 1959 proved to be pivotal in the development of jazz. The relentlessly searching tenor saxophonist John Coltrane recorded *Giant Steps*, an album in which he took the harmonic conventions of bebop established in the late 1940s as far as was possible. He was soon to abandon this approach completely in pursuit of new ideas contained in a recording made in the same year by alto saxophonist Ornette Coleman entitled *The Shape of Jazz to Come*. Coleman's music was often modal or diatonic and relied on linear melodic development rather than harmonic sequences for its structure. His quartet had no chordal instruments and its fluid spontaneity revolutionised the way jazz players thought about harmony and improvisation. *Kind of Blue* by trumpeter Miles Davis, from which *All Blues* is taken, occupies a position somewhere between the two, and was similarly influential.

All Blues

Composed and arranged by Miles Davis. Recorded 22 April 1959 in New York by the Miles Davis Sextet.

Trumpet:	Miles Davis
Alto sax:	Julian 'Cannonball' Adderley
Tenor sax:	John Coltrane
Piano:	Bill Evans
Double bass:	Paul Chambers
Drums:	Jimmy Cobb

Davis was a leading figure of American jazz at this time, and had just completed a groundbreaking series of recordings with composer and arranger Gil Evans, including an innovative recasting of Gershwin's *Porgy and Bess*. For the recordings on *Kind of Blue* Davis reportedly gave the musicians only the briefest of sketches, sometimes just a fragment of a scale, as an indication of the direction of the music. It is usual for jazz musicians to play without detailed written parts if the material is a commonly known standard tune or sequence, but at this time it was a novel way to approach the organisation of original material. Having said that, *All Blues* is one of the more conventional pieces on the record, being a 12-bar blues in G, although its triple metre was novel in jazz at this time.

Time signature and key

Most jazz is improvised, not written down, and attempts to notate it by transcribing recorded performances can take various forms. *All Blues* could be transcribed in 3/4, 6/8 or 6/4. If written in 3/4 the blues sequence would be 24 bars long rather than the more usual 12 bars. In 6/8 we would have a 12-bar sequence but the rhythm would use swung *semi*quavers. The piece is transcribed here in 6/4, keeping the 12-bar sequence and the convention of swung quavers, in order to allow us to make more comparisons with other jazz pieces. In other books you may see extracts printed in 3/4 or 6/8. The chord sequence in *All Blues* is in G, but we have not used a key signature, as the seventh degree of the scale is almost always F♮ rather than F♯.

The pattern of notes G, A, B, C, D, E and F, with G as the home note, is known as the **mixolydian** mode. Unlike G major, it uses F♮, not F♯.

Although triple metre was still relatively new to jazz in 1959, compositions in 'jazz waltz' style, had started to appear in the 1950s. In these, quavers were swung while bass and drums could play either three crotchets per bar ('walking') or a cross-rhythm of two dotted crotchets ('two feel'). Other jazz musicians of the time also experimented with more unusual metres, notably Dave Brubeck who recorded his famous piece in 5/4 time, *Take Five*, in 1959.

Look out for the popular jazz waltz, *It's a Raggy Waltz*, written by Dave Brubeck in 1961.

The arrangement

The head–solos–head format is typical of arrangements for small modern jazz groups when using a repeating chord sequence, the only slight diversion being a four-bar interlude that separates the

---

Warning. Photocopying any part of this book without permission is illegal.

100   All Blues

sections. The 12-bar blues chord sequence is played 19 times (the choruses are numbered in the table, *right*). Note that each of the frontline players are accompanied solely by the rhythm section, as distinct from the Armstrong and Ellington recordings in which the soloists are accompanied by other frontline players. As the harmonic language of jazz became more complex in the 1940s, it became less feasible to use the sort of improvised counterpoint common in New Orleans- and Swing-style jazz, and this practice was gradually abandoned.

The theme

The theme consists of a texture built up from two elements:

✦ a swaying ostinato figure from the saxophones voiced in thirds, underpinned by a one-bar ostinato for bass and supported by a gentle snare-drum pattern played with wire brushes

✦ a piano tremolo and a muted-trumpet melody, both of which take the edge off the clearly-defined rhythms of the ostinato parts.

Form

	Intro	8 bars
1	Theme	12 bars
	Vamp	4 bars
2	Theme repeated	12 bars
	Vamp	4 bars
3–6	Trumpet solo	48 bars
	Vamp	4 bars
7–10	Alto sax solo	48 bars
	Vamp	4 bars
11–14	Tenor sax solo	48 bars
	Vamp	4 bars
15–16	Piano solo	24 bars
	Vamp	4 bars
17	Theme	12 bars
	Vamp	4 bars
18	Theme repeated	12 bars
	Vamp	4 bars
19	Varied repeat and fade-out	

In the first four bars the tonic harmony of G is repeatedly clouded by the F♮ of the mixolydian mode (giving a G^7 chord) and the cluster of notes provided by the piano's tremolo decoration.

In bars 5–6 the alto sax's B♭ changes the chord to Gm^7. This darkens the tone colour without actually moving to chord IV, as would occur in a traditional blues sequence at this point. The saxes mark the change by playing these bars legato and the trumpet moves largely in parallel with them, adding 7ths and 9ths above the alto sax line. Bars 7–8 see a return to the ambiguous tonality of bars 1–4.

At bar 9 a blues sequence normally reaches dominant harmony but here the saxophone notes of C and F above D in the bass produce Dm^7, rather than D major. In bar 10 this voicing slides up a semitone to produce the same sound on E♭, the flattened 6th of the key centre.

Warning. Photocopying any part of this book without permission is illegal.

When reaching chord V in subsequent choruses, pianist Bill Evans uses the C and F but with the addition of an F♯ below (see *left*). Including both the major and minor 3rds of the chord gives a harmonic version of the blues vocal device mentioned in the introduction to these chapters. This voicing is known as a $D^{7\sharp 9}$ (think of F♮ expressed as E♯ to understand why it is a 9th) – well known to rock guitarists as 'the Hendrix chord'.

In the final two bars of the theme the bass ostinato and piano trills return while the frontline play an augmented version of bar one, using dotted minims and simple triadic harmony.

Listening guide

Time	0:00	**Intro**	The eight-bar intro builds up the texture that is going to underpin the theme in the next section. Bass and snare drum (played with wire brushes) outline a simple repeated 6/4 groove, which the pianist decorates with a delicate tremolo. After four bars the saxophones enter, playing a rising and falling ostinato in thirds.
	0:21	**Chorus 1** **Theme**	The theme itself was discussed on the previous page. Miles Davis uses a **harmon mute** for the trumpet solo. This is a metallic mute which normally gives a tight, constricted sound much used for comic effects on cartoon soundtracks. However it has a tube which can be removed from the centre of the mute to give a rather warmer quality, which Davis uses here. This particular way of using the mute, played close to the microphone, was pioneered by Miles Davis and is a hallmark of his distinctive timbre.
	0:53	**Vamp**	Before each new chorus the rhythm section, sometimes augmented by the saxophones, plays a four-bar vamp (see page 81) based on the opening pattern of the intro.
	1:03	**Chorus 2** **Theme repeated**	The theme is repeated, with variations in the trumpet decoration and, in bars 9–10, the new piano harmonies mentioned above.
	1:48	**Choruses 3–6** **Trumpet solo**	At the start of this solo section the sound opens up and begins to expand. The drummer, who till this point has played a repetitive figure on the snare drum with brushes, begins to play on the ride cymbal with sticks. At the same time the piano takes over the backing figure from the saxophones, who stop, and Miles Davis removes the mute to begin his improvisation, which is based on two contrasting ideas:

- in bars 1–4, 7–8 and 11–12 (the chord I bars) of each chorus he uses short, playful rhythmic ideas in mid-range that are mostly based on notes of the underlying triad

- in bars 5–6 (chord I minor) and 9–10 (chords V and ♭VI) he plays lyrical sustained lines, generally in a higher register.

Motifs are short, and constructed from simple materials, but the phrasing shows a highly developed sense of form and proportion. In his first chorus (chorus 3) he develops the 5th to root interval that starts the solo, and then balances this with a descending 3rd to root idea in the next chorus (see *left*). Chorus 5 returns to the 5th to root interval, and his last chorus has a shift in focus to the root an octave higher in combination with the 6th, again creating balance by the use of a descending interval.

All of the bar 9–10 phrases are constructed around the flattened and sharpened 9ths of the V and ♭VI chords. These are played in the upper register, except in chorus 4, where Davis plays them down the octave for variation.

The tonal inflections which Davis achieves are very subtle. His articulation is broad and generally legato and there is very little vibrato, giving a coolness to the sound. He occasionally falls off the pitch of a note (2:16) and uses **ghost notes** (2:23) and **half-valving** (2:29). He also sometimes moves the pitch of long notes around by microtones (3:10) but the use of effects is mainly very sparing.

A **ghost note** is a note that is played almost inaudibly or that is not even sounded at all but merely implied by its context.
Half-valving is the technique of gradually releasing a valve in order to blend one pitch into another. The restricted air flow that this causes also produces a rather nasal tone.

Choruses 7–10   4:01
Alto sax solo

Cannonball Adderley adopts a contrasting approach for his alto sax solo. He begins with phrases consisting mainly of swing quavers and from chorus 8 he introduces quaver triplet and semiquaver runs. The harmonic language is much more chromatic than Davis' diatonic approach and he employs many of the melodic conventions of bebop in his double-time passages (see page 93). There are also many funky blues phrases mixed in with the long bebop lines. Adderley was a virtuoso saxophonist and he covers the whole range of the instrument, moving swiftly from one extreme to the other, again in contrast to the limited range of Davis' phrases. The sound is warm and flexible with a slow vibrato, and he brings rhythmic momentum to his phrasing by emphasising the off-beats.

Choruses 11–14   6:15
Tenor sax solo

John Coltrane's solo has an urgent, forceful character that arises from playing loudly in the upper register of the instrument. He was responsible for greatly extending the technique of the tenor sax and this is reflected in the dextrous repetition and development of short melodic fragments at high speed, answered by chattering snare-drum patterns from Jimmy Cobb. The phrasing alternates between these intense bursts of activity and the decoration of sustained high notes, usually on the 4th or 5th of the key centre.

Two weeks after *All Blues* was made, John Coltrane recorded his influential album *Giant Steps*, which included compositions that moved quickly through many unrelated key centres, and some that stayed entirely within one or two modes. His solo in *All Blues* combines both approaches. He uses minor pentatonic scales and the mixolydian mode for much of the earlier part of the solo, but the chromatic lines in his last two choruses suggest he is thinking of chord substitutions superimposed on the basic tonality.

Choruses 15–16   8:28
Piano solo

The complexity and density of the improvising has so far increased through the solos. In contrast the piano solo reintroduces simple motivic ideas and the use of space. In chorus 15 he plays sustained right-hand notes answered by a delicate left-hand comping figure from the theme. In the chord V and ♭VI bars he follows Davis' approach of a phrase which floats over the pulse, as opposed to the chord I ideas which 'lock in' with the ostinato. Chorus 16 features the development of the comping part into a soloistic idea. Bill Evans uses the rising scalic motif as a right-hand block-chord line, playing it high, mid-range, low and mid-range again. Each of these phrases has a different rhythmic shape, and when Evans repeats the pattern in bars 5–8 he starts to experiment with cross-rhythms and extreme contrasts of articulation. The last four bars wind down gently, with Evans subtly quoting the theme to introduce its return.

Warning. Photocopying any part of this book without permission is illegal.

**9:39 Choruses 17–19
Theme and fade-out**

As at the start, the 12-bar theme is played twice, separated by the four-bar vamp, and with slight variations on the repeat. The vamp is then played one last time to lead into the final chorus, which is a loose repeat during which the track is faded out.

Summary

All Blues was an innovative work, particularly notable for:

- subtle manipulation of texture and timbre
- hypnotic tension through the use of ostinato figures
- an unusual metre for jazz
- interesting harmonic alterations to the basic blues sequence.

In contrast to the other jazz works studied, this is an extended performance of some 11 minutes. The 1950s saw the advent of the 12-inch LP (long play) record which offered 20 minutes of playing time per side. This allowed jazz improvisers to perform in the studio as they would in live performance, enabling them to develop their ideas further than was possible during the three minutes of continuous recording available on earlier types of disc.

Private study

1. What is the mixolydian mode?
2. What is unusual about the metre of *All Blues*?
3. What trumpet effect is particularly associated with Miles Davis?
4. Briefly outline two different approaches to solo improvisation heard in *All Blues*.

Group work

Improvising

Put the recording on and tap the crotchet pulse on your right leg with your right hand as you listen to the saxophone figure. Then add a dotted-crotchet pulse with your left hand on your left leg as you listen to the bass, as shown *left*. You may find it useful to think of the words 'nice cup of tea' to help coordinate the rhythms. Try this pattern out on two different percussion instruments or on the piano, with a two-note bass line and a three-beat comping part in the right hand. Use this idea as an ostinato in your own lead-sheet arrangement. Also try using Miles Davis' technique of adding 9ths (diatonic or occasionally chromatic) to basic chord progressions.

Further reading

See also 'Further Reading' on page 98.

Miles Davis Kind of Blue: Transcribed Scores. *Hal Leonard*. ISBN: 0-6340-1169-3. This contains transcriptions of the tracks on *Kind of Blue*, including *All Blues*.

Kind of Blue by Ashley Kahn. Published September 2000 in the USA by *Da Capo Press*. ISBN: 0-306-80986-9. To be published in the UK in March 2001 by *Granta Books*. ISBN: 1-86207-424-0. This book promises a very detailed account of the recording of the album.

Selected discography

At the time of going to press OCR was planning to issue its own CD of the prescribed jazz works to include the specified version of this piece.

Kind of Blue, Miles Davis. *Sony Jazz CK64935*. The original album. This CD can be used, on a suitably equipped computer, with an on-line presentation about *Kind of Blue*, to be found at the website http://www.sonymusic.com/thelab/ConnecteD/MilesDavis/

Look out for **Giant Steps**, John Coltrane. *Atlantic 8122752032*. Coltrane's influential 1959 recording in which he extended the boundaries of harmonic complexity and technical control. Also **Sketches of Spain**, Miles Davis. *Sony Jazz CK65142*. A large scale work which stretched the formal and harmonic conventions of jazz and, along with *Kind of Blue*, introduced modal improvisation.

Further listening

Aural practice

The skeleton score printed below shows parts of the trumpet solo in chorus 3 of *All Blues*. Listen to this music as many times as you need while you answer the questions which follow.

This extract will be found between timings 1:48 and 2:16 on the CD.

1. Describe the effect used on the notes marked **X** (bars 2 and 12). ....
2. Bars 1–4 are centred on a G^7 chord. What is the chord in bars 5–6? ....
3. Complete the trumpet part in bar 4 and bars 7–8. The rhythm of bar 4 is shown above the stave.
4. What is played by the drummer in this extract? ....
5. How does the chord marked **Y** relate to the first chord in bar 10? ....
6. Describe as precisely as possible the key or mode of this extract. ....

Question practice

1. Compare the use of the 12-bar blues in *All Blues* with the use of the same pattern in **either** *West End Blues* **or** *Ko-ko*.
2. Briefly describe three contrasting techniques of improvisation, using examples from the three jazz works you have studied.
3. Why is Miles Davis regarded as such an important figure in the development of modern jazz?
4. What is meant by the term 'modal jazz'?
5. In what ways did the newly developing technology of recording affect jazz?

Warning. Photocopying any part of this book without permission is illegal.

All Blues 105

> Prescribed for examination in 2003 and 2004

Straight No Chaser — Monk/Evans (1959)

Canadian-born Gil Evans (1912–88) was a self-taught pianist and arranger whose most influential and innovative contribution to jazz was in his collaborations with trumpeter Miles Davis. His first well-known professional work was as chief arranger for the Claude Thornhill Band in the mid 1940s. This big band used unconventional instrumentation, including two french horns and a tuba, and played with very little vibrato. Evans said,

> 'the sound of the band was almost a reduction to an inactivity of music, to a stillness ... The sound hung like a cloud.'

The experience of working with this group broadened the range of tone colour and texture that Evans was to use in his later work.

Gil Evans went on to become a central figure in the development of the Miles Davis Nonet recordings of 1949, known as *The Birth Of The Cool* sessions, from which the track *Move* is taken. In the late 1950s Evans and Davis reunited for a series of ground-breaking albums including his innovative recasting of Gershwin's *Porgy and Bess*, which established Evans as a leading arranger in American jazz. *Straight No Chaser* comes from an album called *Great Jazz Standards* that he made between his Miles Davis projects in 1959, and in which he gives unusual and individual twists to well known jazz compositions.

The original theme

Pianist and composer Thelonious Monk first recorded *Straight No Chaser* in 1952 and it was subsequently recorded by the Miles Davis Sextet in 1958. To the present day it has remained a standard 12-bar blues head played by jazz musicians worldwide. Monk was an eccentric and unorthodox figure whose music was appreciated by other jazz musicians, but not initially understood by critics or the public. His compositions and improvising are characterised by:

- use of dissonance, including chord clusters
- unusual rhythmic construction and irregularly placed accents
- repetition of melodic fragments, often rhythmically displaced.

These elements can be heard in the theme of *Straight No Chaser*, and also in Gil Evans' Monk-like piano solos, as we shall see later.

The arrangement

Gil Evans' arrangement has an unusual frontline. The conventional big band line-up developed during the 1930s and 1940s had sections of trumpets, trombones and saxophones, with three or four players in each. In creating a group specifically to record these pieces Evans opted for an ensemble consisting primarily of brass: three trumpets and three trombones, augmented by french horn and tuba. In addition there is Steve Lacy's soprano sax, used mainly as a solo voice, and an alto sax which is distantly heard in the intro and coda. The resulting texture is much smoother and more homogeneous than that of a swing band with a large saxophone section.

The other striking feature of this arrangement is the way that Evans avoids the big-band convention of scoring in parallel block chords,

---

The word 'straight' in the title refers to an undiluted alcoholic drink such as a whisky without water. A 'chaser' is a contrasting drink, such as a beer to follow the whisky. 'Straight No Chaser' (a phrase uttered by many a hard drinker in American movies of the day) therefore implies an intense, undiluted experience.

Straight No Chaser

Original version for piano by Thelonious Monk (1952). This version arranged by Gil Evans. Recorded early 1959 in New York by the Gil Evans Orchestra.

Trumpets:	Johnny Coles
	Louis Mucci
	Allen Smith
Trombones:	Curtis Fuller
	Bill Elton
	Dick Lieb
French horn:	Bob Northern
Tuba:	Bill Barber
Soprano sax:	Steve Lacy
Reeds:	Al Block
Piano:	Gil Evans
Guitar:	Chuck Wayne
Double bass:	Dick Carter
Drums:	Dennis Charles

as used by Ellington in *Ko-ko*. The established formula in this style was to voice the sections of the band in triadic harmony, often coloured by chromatic passing chords. In essence the choice of chords dictated the character of the instrumental lines in this style. Evans preferred a more linear approach, in which it is the contrapuntal combination of melodies that defines the resulting chords.

Listening guide

Straight No Chaser is based on 27 choruses of a medium tempo blues sequence shown on page 68.

The piece begins with the bass adopting a conventional walking pattern while the drummer plays time on the ride cymbal. However instead of comping in the usual way, the pianist and guitarist play trills in a very high register to create the static cloud of sound of which Evans was so fond. In the second chorus Evans begins the angular, jerky piano interjections which resurface at various points in the piece. The saxophone line introduced in the second chorus suggests a minor key, focusing as it does on the 2nd and minor 3rd.

Monk's relentlessly ascending theme is now presented in its original form, scored in octaves, with none of the big-band convention of parallel block chords:

Form		
1–2	Intro	24 bars
3–4	Theme	24 bars
5–8	Trumpet solo	48 bars
9–11	Soprano sax solo	36 bars
12–14	Trombone solo	36 bars
15–18	Piano solo	48 bars
19–23	Theme	60 bars
24–27	Coda leading to fade-out	

Choruses 1–2 Time 0:00
Intro

Choruses 3–4 0:29
Theme

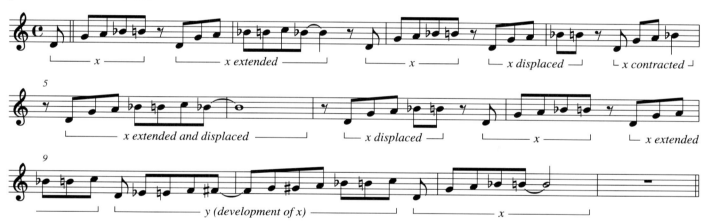

The melody centres around the contrast between the minor 3rd (B♭) and the major 3rd (B♮). This is a classic blues device, but one which is transformed by Monk's unerring sense of motivic development and rhythmic versatility. The initial five-note motif (*x*) is extended, contracted and displaced in rhythm to different beats of the bar. The extended version is itself displaced in bar 5, and in bar 9 the chromatic ending of the extended version is taken as the basis for *y*, a climbing chromatic phrase which starts with the rhythm of *x* and that neatly brings us back to the original motif.

Monk uses the AAB blues convention of establishing an idea in the first four bars, reusing it in the next four, and then introducing new material in the last four bars. However he subtly disguises the 12-bar form by the shifting of phrases and the close relationship of the new idea to the previous idea. Notice how phrases almost invariably end with off-beat accents, highlighted by cymbal strokes. This is a typical jazz device to anticipate changes of harmony and move the music forward. In the repeat of the theme (chorus 4) the frontline arrangement stays the same, but the piano adds some crunchy, dissonant chords in response to the melodic phrases.

| 0:58 | **Choruses 5–8**
 Trumpet solo | Johnny Coles' understated lyrical style is heavily influenced by the language of bebop and the playing of Miles Davis (compare this solo with Davis' solo in *Move*). The main characteristics are: |

- long lines consisting primarily of swing quaver patterns
- a rich harmonic vocabulary that uses complex chords
- highly decorated phrases with many chromatic passing notes
- quotations of old popular songs, such as *Don't Sit Under the Apple Tree* (at 1:27) and *Thanks For The Memory* (at 1:40).

His trumpet sound is soft and warm, and the swing quavers have a legato feel. He subtly employs melodic decoration such as the turns which decorate the motif with which he begins his solo. He also likes to smear the 5th with half-valving (see page 103). This can be heard at the approximate timings 1:30 and 1:39.

Coles begins in a simple and spacious way, transposing his initial idea when the harmony moves up to the subdominant. It is then repeated in the tonic before he introduces a new idea in the last four bars. This is another example of the classic AAB formula for constructing blues melodies.

In chorus 6 the piano drops out and the trumpet line becomes more fluid rhythmically but also more oblique harmonically, with Coles choosing to end his long eight-bar phrase on C♯ (1:21), thus introducing a sound that is to recur in the written arrangement. He then revisits the flat 5th at the end of the following phrase.

The tension created by this note is released at the beginning of chorus 7, with the consonant, diatonic nature of his *Apple Tree* quote. The simplicity of this idea is soon balanced with more complex chromatic material.

A similar pattern of a diatonic idea quickly followed by chromatic material is used in the final trumpet chorus, which ends in an unresolved way, again centred around the flat 5th of the key.

| 1:54 | **Choruses 9–11**
 Soprano sax solo | There is no prearranged material during the trumpet and soprano saxophone solos, other than the basic blues pattern, but notice how the pianist subtly alters the texture by: |

- resting in the two middle choruses of the trumpet solo
- resting in the first and third choruses of the soprano sax solo.

Steve Lacy's soprano sax solo is more closely related to the theme of *Straight No Chaser* than Johnny Coles' improvisation. His sound is full and particularly strong in the upper register and he adopts a legato approach to fast moving lines similar to that of Coles.

Lacy's initial idea is centred around G, B♭ and B♮ and is derived from the theme. This is one of the few phrases in the solo which is articulated rather than slurred. It is next contrasted with a sweeping scalic figure which settles on low chord tones. The theme is then quoted and developed in the last four bars.

The final phrase of chorus 9 is resolved on the first beat of chorus 10, and Lacy continues with an ascending and descending phrase in which again he adapts the theme (at 2:09). The last four bars sees the introduction of a D–C♯ idea that is a reference to a backing we are yet to hear, a clever device which unifies the improvised and composed elements in the same way as his use of the theme in his solo.

Chorus 10, bars 8–12

In his final chorus (chorus 11) Lacy moves quickly across the range of the instrument, repeating ideas in different octaves. The D–C♯ pattern is incorporated into the upward-moving gesture we have heard in each of the previous choruses and is now in the top register. He descends scalically and begins winding down to end the solo. The final few bars see two more fleeting appearances of the theme (at 2:30 and 2:36) before the overlap into the next solo.

A change in texture is achieved in chorus 12 by the introduction of a comping pattern from guitar and the arrival of the backing figure mentioned earlier, played by muted trumpets and low brass:

Choruses 12–14 2:36
Trombone solo

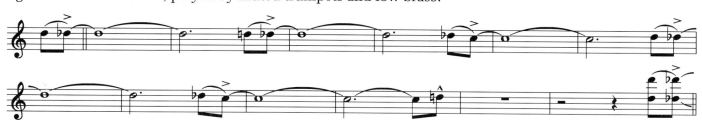

This strong, blues-influenced pattern gives the trombonist something to play off without crowding the solo rhythmically. When this backing is repeated, the soprano sax joins an octave above the trumpets, who make an interesting rasping sound by the combined use of harmon mutes (see page 102) and **flutter tonguing**.

Flutter tonguing involves the player rolling an 'r' while producing the notes.

Curtis Fuller's trombone solo employs much of the same bebop phrasing as the trumpet solo, but differs in the use of:

- predominantly diatonic and pentatonic melodic ideas
- quaver triplets to give momentum
- a more robust, percussive delivery.

Fuller's approach is cleaner than that of many swing trombonists, in that he doesn't use the slide to produce obvious effects. However we do hear occasional falls in pitch at the end of emphatic phrase endings, and a great deal of sliding between the notes B and C. There is also much variety of articulation; we hear legato swing quavers as in the previous solos, but also some heavily attacked short notes and rapid double-time articulation known as 'doodle tonguing'.

Fuller anticipates the beginning of chorus 12, overlapping with Steve Lacy in the process, and settles on the tonic in bar 1 of the sequence with a three-note rhythmic motif. He repeats this idea in bar 5, but moves up in pitch to B♭. There follow some accented, percussive notes in imitation of the choppy guitar comping. These lead into a longer, more dense phrase dominated by scalic triplet quaver runs.

Chorus 13 starts with an emphatic tonic, an octave higher than the G which began the previous chorus, and with a fall in pitch at the end. Fuller responds to the entry of the backing figure with long lines, based on swing quavers, higher in the trombone range.

Warning. Photocopying any part of this book without permission is illegal.

In his final chorus Fuller leaves space in the first few bars as the backing figure repeats with increased intensity. He responds with blues-inflected phrases that use the minor pentatonic scale, and then a fast climactic phrase (at 3:13) based on sextuplets. The final phrase leads us back to the repeated use of the tonic on the first bar of the next chorus, as in the first and second choruses.

3:18 **Choruses 15–18 Piano solo**

Having increased the density and dynamic of the piece during the trombone solo, the level of activity drops back down to something close to the beginning of the piece. Gil Evans' playing is heavily influenced by that of Thelonious Monk. His first two choruses use mainly single-line melodic improvisation, while the remaining two feature chordal playing which sounds almost like a comping part. The key characteristics of the solo are:

- extensive use of space to frame musical events
- the development of simple melodic and rhythmic motifs
- a modal approach in which Evans repeats the same ideas over the different harmonies of the sequence.

After the intensity of the final trombone chorus Evans cools things down by employing the simplest of melodic ideas based around just a few pitches. His touch is light and percussive, and the sparse ideas leave ample room for the high bass part to be heard.

There is an increased level of activity in chorus 16, and the introduction of the left hand to fill out the texture. The final four bars sees the introduction of parallel 6ths in the right hand that moves us toward the chordal playing to come.

In chorus 17 Evans plays percussive figures to harmonise a two note idea around D and E. This static melodic idea is in contrast to the scalic nature of the preceeding choruses and the theme to come.

In his final chorus Evans extends this static idea to include the ubiquitous flat 5th (C♯/D♭). This leads to dissonant, jagged chords underpinned by the rumbling of some very low piano notes. Here Evans is exploring the sonority of the instrument rather than taking a functional harmonic approach.

4:13 **Choruses 19–23 Theme**

Evans extends the theme over five choruses, gradually thickening the texture and creating interest by introducing contrapuntal ideas and manipulating the dynamic levels.

Chorus 19 recapitulates the theme in octaves, but with the added weight of the tuba at the bottom of the texture. In the following chorus the melody is harmonised at the third above by soprano sax. This draws attention to the harmony part, making it sound almost like a new lead line. At this point the listener is also engaged by the drop in the dynamic level.

Chorus 22 sees a further drop in dynamic and at the same time a thickening of the texture by the use of an inversion of the theme in the trumpets. This descending line balances the ascending nature of the original theme and its soprano sax harmonisation.

Two major changes occur in chorus 22. The soprano sax moves up to a higher register, playing the original theme an octave above the trumpets. This opening of the range in the scoring has an emphatic effect which is tempered by the introduction of the dissonant long note backing figure from the trombone solo providing a strong contrast to the ever moving rhythm of the theme. Chorus 23 repeats the brass writing, but soprano sax and piano improvise – not in a soloistic fashion but to add to the various different layers building up, helping to make this the climactic point of the piece.

The coda returns to the texture of the intro, with piano and guitar high in their ranges. In chorus 25 Evans adds a jaunty touch with blues and boogie-woogie clichés, transforming them by using a very high register and adding piquant clashes. The return of the alto sax figure based on the 2nd and minor 3rd darkens the tonality and acts as a foil to the brightness of the high piano in the major key, which continues until the fadeout.

Choruses 24–27 5:23
Coda and fadeout

Private study

1. What is unusual about the instrumentation of this work?
2. Which aspects of Gil Evans' piano playing in *Straight No Chaser* were influenced by Thelonious Monk?
3. Briefly state what is meant by motivic development.
4. How does Gil Evans provide variety in a piece that consists of 27 repetitions of the same harmonic pattern?

Composing

Look again at the music example on page 107 and notice how the extension, development and displacement of a short motif gives rhythmic interest and avoids the predictability that can arise from too much four-bar phrasing. Try using this technique in your own lead-sheet arrangement. It will be easier if you devise a motif that is very short and based on a strong pattern, such as notes from the tonic chord, linked by a few passing notes. You may be able to find a suitable motif in the tune you are arranging. Try using a backing pattern like the one on page 109. Notice its main characteristics: a harmony note held for seven beats, then brief rhythmic movement in which the next long note is anticipated by an accented quaver. Don't use this precise rhythm, but try to adopt a similarly minimal approach in which sparingly few notes are used to maximum effect.

Further reading

Jazz Arranging and Composing: A Linear Approach by Bill Dobbins. *Rottenburg/Advance Music*, 1986. ISBN: 3-89221-006-3. This has a detailed study of Evans' contrapuntal style of arranging.

Selected discography

Gil Evans Orchestra, *Giants Of Jazz 53158*. This includes the Gil Evans version of *Straight No Chaser*. The original album *Great Jazz Standards* has been deleted from the CD catalogues.

The Best of Thelonious Monk, *Blue Note CDP 7956362*. This CD includes the rather idiosyncratic original version by the composer.
Milestones, Miles Davis. *Columbia 4608272*. Another version of *Straight No Chaser*, by the Miles Davis Sextet of the late 1950s.

At the time of going to press OCR was planning to issue its own CD of the prescribed jazz works to include the specified version of this piece.

Further listening

Warning. Photocopying any part of this book without permission is illegal.

Aural practice

This extract will be found between timings 0:58 and 1:14 on the CD.

The skeleton score printed below shows parts of the trumpet solo in chorus 5 of *Straight No Chaser*. Listen to this music as many times as you need while you answer the questions which follow.

1. Complete the bass part in bars 1 and 2.
2. How does the trumpet part in bar 6 relate to the motif heard in bar 4? ....
3. How does the trumpet part in bars 7–8 relate to this same motif? ....
4. Complete the missing bass notes indicated by the bracket in bars 9–10.
5. Complete the trumpet part in bar 11.
6. What name is given to this type of bass part? ....
7. Briefly describe what is played by the pianist in this passage ....
   .... and what is played by the drummer. ....

 Question practice

1. Does the arrangement of *Straight No Chaser* succeed in giving a new lease of life to the traditional format of a 12-bar blues?

2. Briefly describe three contrasting techniques of improvisation, using examples from the three jazz works you have studied.

3. Compare the relationship between composed and improvised material in **either** *Rockin' In Rhythm* **or** *Straight No Chaser*.

4. How does the use of motivic development in *Straight No Chaser* compare with the use of this technique in the first movement of Mozart's Piano Concerto in A, K488.

5. To what extent do you think that Gil Evans was influenced by Duke Ellington in his style of instrumentation?

Warning. Photocopying any part of this book without permission is illegal.

112 Straight No Chaser